THE CULTURE *of* MONEY

THE CULTURE *of* MONEY

DE'ANDRE SALTER

The Culture of Money
Copyright © 2020 by De'Andre Salter

Published by Mynd Matters Publishing
715 Peachtree Street NE, Suites 100 & 200, Atlanta, GA 30308

Books may be purchased in quantity and/or special sales by contacting the author.

ISBN 978-1-953307-11-8 (Pbk)
ISBN 978-1-953307-12-5 (hdcv)
ISBN 978-1-953307-12-5 (Ebook)

Library of Congress Control Number: 2020921407

First Edition

For my wife Terri and my children Dejahn, Destiny, Dorian, and Davin, without whom this book would have no reason. Their motivation, love, and support gave me the strength to pursue wealth, leave a legacy, and serve the world. Family is everything.

CONTENTS

INTRODUCTION

"The first step to controlling your world is to control your culture... To write the books. Make the music. Shoot the films. Paint the art."
—Chuck Palahniuk

The economic outlook for Black people in America is bleak. There is an economic tsunami heading directly toward Black America and it will hit in approximately 25 years. Like any natural disaster, this economic one will widen an already cavernous wealth gap and potentially wipe out Black wealth. No one living then will escape it. The game will change in a major way.

In 20 years, a 25-year-old today will be 45, and find himself with meager resources available to build a business, retire early or leave a legacy – unless he takes this issue seriously, changes his behaviors, makes a plan and executes it.

In 20 years, a 45-year-old today will be 65 and find himself in a situation where he can't leave a viable financial legacy. He will leave a legacy of lack. Meanwhile, his White and Asian peers will be bragging about the incredible accomplishments and prospects available to their heirs.

We can't stop storms. They happen. However, we can prepare for storms, survive and perhaps even thrive in them. The government cannot and will not be the sole solution to the economic tsunami I am writing about. We don't even have the political capital to make it so even if it was possible. This storm will have to be dealt with in the manner of most storms—in each home. The response will require leadership in an unprecedented way. A money movement. An economic revolution in Black America will do its best to lessen the effects of the greatest wealth transfer in world history.

So, while this is a book about Black money, it is not a regurgitation of the financial advice that many listen to from people who do not value the Black economic experience. I will not insult you by telling you, "Simply build an emergency savings fund as your first step toward financial freedom." That would completely ignore the context of why it's so difficult for the average Black person to save.

This book will change the way you think about your finances. It is written for *you*, family. It will help you wake up and learn how money has affected your past, is a driving force in your quality of life today and will be the largest determinant of your future lifestyle. It will help you make money moves.

The Culture of Money Is Black Alignment

Alignment allows you to make a much stronger case for change right from the beginning. *The culture of money* is an economic ideology for all Black individuals to *know more, own more and pass down more.* We need to align ourselves around these three simple, action-oriented, values to save our future. *The culture of money* is an old concept with roots far beyond the post-plantation money culture birthed after the Civil War that Blacks largely abandoned. It is time for members of the Black community to reclaim a more viable money culture in order to truly live the dream of their forefathers.

Following the American Civil War, during the reconstruction period in 1867 – 1877, Black Wall Streets arose in places like Tulsa, Rosewood, FL and Harlem. They were aligned around the same values–*know more, own more and pass down more*. They became the meccas of Black enterprise, Black property ownership and the way to secure means for Black families to prosper for generations. Their goal was legacy. The dominant culture did not admire but rather scoffed at Black success as realistically depicted in the first episode of *The Watchmen* HBO series.

Presently, things have shifted. Black culture is no longer abhorred but widely mimicked. Today Blacks have more cultural influence than any other generation EXCEPT when it comes to money. Beyond an exceptional few who have made major fortunes, Blacks are often the laughingstock of others. Many outsiders view Blacks as a people who are only consumed with "flash" and "wearing their wealth on their backs." In many eyes, Blacks are the agents of their own financial ruin, even though that is the furthest thing from the truth.

The culture of money is Black America's awakening and realignment. It is shifting the narrative toward a positive money culture. It is Black goals restored. This simple platform focuses on individual behavior changes, so that collectively Blacks can start living the blessed life. We can't control outcomes but we can control our behaviors so that we can become prosperous. *The culture of money* is faith-based. To get the alignment we need a great deliverance must happen and the Black church must take a leadership position.

Churches, schools, Black enterprises and nonprofits that embrace this ideology will be in the best position to help their patrons re-center their lives around managing money based upon these three simple values. The institutions that become part of the solution will benefit the most from the increased wealth and generosity within our community, thus providing them with sustainability.

The economic tsunami I spoke of earlier refers to a $68 trillion transfer of wealth happening by 2045. This means there will be an entirely new group of individuals ruling the realm of the elite. However how many of those people will be us, those who make up the Black communities of America?

Most reports estimate only 3% of this transfer of generational wealth will be seen in the homes of Black Americans. So, while Blue Ivy, Christian Combs, North West, Diggy Simmons and other celebrity youth will have a large amount of money coming to them, what about your kids and mine? Think about it. If you are twenty now, you will be forty-five then and probably not inheriting any money while your White and Asian peers inherit more power and privilege. If you are forty now, you will be sixty-five then and probably not in position to transfer any wealth unless you become *the culture of money* today!

Don't worry; I'm not going to write a book about statistics. But you've got to admit that the 3% figure is disturbing. Think about it. This great wealth transfer will be an economic tsunami that hurts us bad. What will you do to make sure that you survive the implications? What will you do to make sure that the loved ones who come up after you have a financial head start? How will they have a fighting chance in a society where most of the wealth will be in the hands of "other" people?

What if you are in your 20s and just beginning your income years or you are in your 30s and just starting a family? You might not want to focus on passing down wealth. Maybe your only concern is your student loan debt, your mortgage or buying diapers and formula. I'm here to wake you up! The giant money wave is going to take you out in your 40s and you will regret not doing more earlier.

These are not questions solely for old Black people to answer. Every college-aged Black adult and beyond must get aligned with the culture of money.

You, too, must become *the culture of money.* Sure, you're young now, but one day you won't be. You get to decide <u>right now</u> how you will want to live as an older person – happy and woke or miserable and broke! Have the foresight to understand what the future holds: a financial tsunami that might wipe out and eliminate Black wealth.

It's possible that you are the only one who might be able to provide a better Black legacy. Or, will you be the reason that the next generation falls even further behind? That choice was what drove me to success in my 20s and why my estate is set up to ensure my kids are on the winning side of that wealth transfer.

The Culture of Money Is Biblical

I've worked hard, followed God's plan and principles so that my legacy will be positive. I've written *The Culture of Money* for people who are serious about family, faith and finances. You believe money begets power and power begets money. You believe faith works and you work your faith.

The culture of money is for those who embrace godly wisdom. Please know it is God's will that you wake up and start living *the culture of money*.

Proverbs 13:22 says, *"Good people leave an inheritance to their grandchildren, but a sinner's wealth is stored up for good people."* Yes, I'm a bishop, but this is a different type of altar call. I'm calling you to the altar of financial healing. This text reveals it is God's desire/will to manage your money properly. This is a revelation about what you are supposed to do with your money if you are "good people." It gives us financial purpose. In this passage, the person who is good is the one who has a life goal to transfer wealth. The sinner wastes money and is easily taken advantage of by those who *know more*. So family, if you were to die today, which part of the text would best describe you?

Blacks need a sense of urgency to adopt *the culture of money* so that they won't be left outside of God's more excellent plan and on the wrong side of history.

The Culture of Money Is Empowering

An ideology expresses dissatisfaction with the current state of things and sets aspirations toward a better future.[1] *The culture of money* is an empowerment ideology aimed at changing the financial future of Black people.

The culture of money is the basis for financial healing that results in behavioral shifts, specifically in how Black people view, use and manage money. If you need to *know more* than the fact that $68 trillion will be changing hands over the next 25 years and our people may not get their fair share of it, then I send my thoughts and prayers. Blacks cannot solely rely on public policy or reparations to solve this issue for their individual families.

I charge you, the readers of this book, to get your financial healing and to walk in the new financial behaviors necessary and spread *the culture of money* in your home, church, community groups and social organizations. It is the heart of God for Black people. We are the culture. Live it. Be it. Control it. Be *the culture of money*.

As I mentioned before, this book is not safe. If you don't want a deliverance, then close this book now! I'm partnering with the open-minded who want to be challenged to adopt a better, more faithful way to prosper. I plan to share the truth; you will only read about what you can become, not what you can't accomplish. To do so, this book may examine some of the situations you have experienced in your financial past so you can make a better path to where you are heading. Only continue if you are ready to experience multiple breakthroughs. Prepare to act!

ONE

We Need The Culture of Money

'll let you in on a little secret – you must have motivation to make any change. Some people are moved by negative motivators like fear, or positive motivators like dreams, a loved one, or a deep faith.

It may seem unorthodox to start a book with questions, but they are necessary for you to emotionally, mentally and spiritually buy in to a future that will be possible if you embrace *the culture of money*. For now, let's motivate ourselves by visioning.

Let's imagine that tomorrow morning you woke up and suddenly inherited $1 million. What would be the first thing you'd do? Buy a brand-new car or a complete wardrobe? Pay off student loans? Take a bucket-list vacation? Start a business? Quit your job? Bless your momma with a new house? Pay for your kids' college education? Donate generously to your church? Bless all those people who have blessed you in the past? Or, maybe invest the money so you can leave a healthy inheritance?

Any one of these options sound great. Think about what

it would feel like to have financial fitness and less stress. Or how it would feel to be the blessor rather than the one who always needs a blessing. Consider the impact you can have on others by becoming a wealth role model in your family, church or community, because let's face it...of all the testimonies that move people, financial success is a big draw.

Right now, you may have a professional career, a nice job and a side hustle, but can you make any or all the dreams I mentioned come true? Are you financially free or bound? Do you have a future proof financial plan? If not, don't worry; you are not alone. According to a recent study, only one in 10 Blacks do financial planning with a professional.

The culture of money is agreeing to live by three simple principles: *know more, own more and pass down more*! If you follow these principles, most, if not all, of your dreams could become possible. Keep reading to find out how.

Houston, We Have a Problem

I wasn't born into a family of generational wealth and our financial knowledge was limited. While attending school, including college, I don't remember having any classes that dealt with money. Both of my parents worked their butts off to educate and raise five kids in Newark, NJ. But the truth is, they had never attended any financial education classes either. Everything they had learned was primarily through the school of trial and error. The same pattern holds true for my grandparents and great grandparents. I'm certain that very few of my ancestors born on the plantation in Damascus, Georgia were ever taught wealth-building principles.

Blacks are a people who have generationally learned through experience and watching how others managed their money. *And therein lies the problem.* If no one in the home is well informed and the schools don't cover the subject of finances and the only teaching on money in church is about generosity, where does that leave us? With generations handing down misinformation, misguidance and poor money-handling skills?

Let's take it a step further. What if most of the experiences you've had with money have been associated with negativity, crisis or traumatic events? Here are a few examples you or your family members may have experienced: scrambling for enough money to pay for a loved one's funeral; dodging bill collectors with the famous line, "He ain't here" or loaning money to broke relatives so they won't get evicted. Sound familiar?

What if most of the people you watched managed their money poorly or not at all? What if you never had exposure to a single wealthy person in your whole life? What if most of the people you knew tried their best, but they were born so far underwater that they could never escape a crisis-filled life themselves? What if you primarily went to church with people who always needed a financial blessing and could rarely bless others? No, this is not the entirety of the Black experience, but it is mine and perhaps yours. The fact is that many Blacks are born into this exact situation.

Traditional Budgeting Advice Is Not Black Enough

Most books and programs about money, personal finance and budgeting don't resonate with Black individuals because they miss the point and are tone-deaf to our situation. Many of these books provide the same advice that is right in principle, but the authors don't always know what many members of the Black community go through. Some of us may be able to adhere to their steps to *financial freedom*, but others can't.

Many of these other books say you must save more money and live on a budget while they completely ignore the fact Black Americans are still often the last hired and first fired. This is not an excuse, just a reality, which means lower overall incomes for Blacks is a bigger contributor to their scarcity of wealth than poor budgeting.

Following financial guidelines to start simply by building an emergency fund equal to three months of your salary is ludicrous and tone-deaf when:

- Black income is half that of White households in the US – just like it was in the 1950s[1]
- Black unemployment is historically double that of Whites, even in the best of times[2]
- Blacks with college degrees are twice as likely to be unemployed as other graduates[3]
- A Black college student has the same chances of getting a job as a White high school dropout[4]

How are you supposed to magically save up money from a job where you may earn 50% less than your White counterparts? And even though you might be better educated, you are more likely to lose your job or become unemployed or underemployed compared to them?

Let's slam the door shut on the argument that while an emergency savings fund might be a good place to start, it is a premature place because that goal is not as easily attainable and feasible for Blacks. *The culture of money* moves you to *know more, own more and pass down more.* We shall overcome the stats and get ahead by changing our behaviors.

People are always singled out for their spending and Black people more than many others. The customary solution is that budgeting will solve your problems. So, how has that worked out for you? Trying to solve an income problem by cutting expenses is pointless. It's like trying to put a square peg in a round hole. Let's agree that while budgeting is a necessary evil, Black people as a whole don't make enough money.

Living within a smaller income is a bigger problem than living within a budget. And what about those people who *know* they don't have enough money yet *still* use the little wealth they have to purchase expensive cars and flashy designer stuff? Let's hope they will come around eventually once enough of us show them a more excellent way.

The up-and-coming Black professionals who are making a decent income but still have very little wealth to show for it need to make the shift first. You have means, access and potential to do this and become a money mentor for others.

Now, let's get back to the argument and show why you feel like no matter what you do to try to get ahead, it's not enough. Did that get your attention? I thought it would. But if even that wasn't enough, how about this:

- Your situation is not entirely of your own making
- You've been fed outdated information – not knowingly and not intentionally – but completely irrelevant to today's economy
- The economy doesn't work the way it used to, so neither can you

Over the course of this chapter, I will dissect these points to show you why each is true and what happened in our society and in our economy to make them true. You will come to understand that the way you view and budget your money has to change if you have any intentions of staying on top of things financially.

As you read, I want you to pause now and then to think about how the facts, stats and figures in front of you play out in your own life. I'm going to continue throwing in a few questions now and then that I hope will make you stop and think about your current situation and what you want your future to look like. By doing so, you will be able to better relate to what is on the page and use it to bring about positive changes to your financial situation and outlook.

Back in the day when your grandparents and even your parents were starting their grownup lives, they did not bring a lot of baggage with them—baggage by the name of debt. They didn't bring student loan debt, or if they did, it wasn't much. They didn't have credit card bills to pay each month (with interest) and they certainly weren't making payments on a mobile phone. If anything, they had a small car note. If they were lucky, they were able to put a down payment on a house within the first few years of their marriage, making the mortgage payment their only real debt.

Today that is simply not the case. According to facts and figures from studentloanhero.com:

- 66% of graduates from public colleges had loans averaging $25,550
- 75% of graduates from private nonprofit colleges had loans with an average balance of $32,300
- 88% of graduates from for-profit colleges had loans in the amount of $39,950

Those amounts are more than most of your grandparents would have paid for a house or a car. They probably didn't spend that much on their education if they went to college. The budgeting principles that worked for them probably won't work for you unless you started life as a grown-up without any debt. But why not? Why doesn't a budget that operates on the principles of adjusting your expenses to fit your income work? Here's why: economy and spending habits.

This Is Not Grandma's Economy Anymore

I know statistics can be boring and even confusing at times, but I would like you to take a look at these figures. They are the best way to help you realize why traditional budgeting isn't working for most Black people anymore.

According to the National Department of Labor, the hourly minimum wage in 1974 was $1.90. In 1979 it was $2.90; in 1996 it was $4.75; in 2009 it was $7.25; and today, it varies by state. But by and large, most states remain at $7.25 per hour. This is the wage paid for jobs held by people working in retail, food service, cashiers and other traditionally low-level employment opportunities.

According to the same report, the average hourly earnings for production and non-supervisory employees has grown from $13.21 in December 1998 to $22.30 in December 2017 for factory workers, teachers, delivery truck and warehouse employees and people working in service-oriented jobs like bank tellers and receptionists.

If you do the math, you will see that the low-level blue-collar jobs are paying four times as much now as they were in 1974 and wages have nearly doubled for those working in jobs that require more skill and training. That sounds somewhat impressive, but unfortunately, it isn't. The reason? The increase in pay has not kept up with the increase in the cost of goods and services considered necessary and normal for every American household. For example, look at how costs have increased over the years[5]:

- Average yearly income: in 1975 – $12,686; in 2015 – $51,759
- Average cost to build a new house: in 1975 – $48,000; in 2015 – $270,200
- Average cost for a new car: in 1975 – $3,800; in 2015 – $31,200
- Average cost for a year in public (state) university: in 1975 – $1,819; in 2015 – $18,943 for the same university
- Average cost for a gallon of gas: in 1975 – $.59; in 2015 – between $2.38 and $3.55
- Average cost of a gallon of milk: in 1975 – $1.65; in 2015 – $3.49

Don't rush pass these figures; stop a minute to look at the changes in the cost of things. The average yearly income went up quite a bit. But did it really? The average income rose a little over $39,000, but the average cost of a house rose over $222,000.

It doesn't really matter how you look at it. The ability to make house payments making an hourly minimum wage just isn't there. Here's why: in 1975, a 30-year mortgage on a $48,000 house cost the home buyer $330 a month – Principal and Interest (P&I). A $270,200 30-year mortgage with the same terms cost the homeowner $1,680 a month (P&I). That means with an average monthly salary of around $1,000 in 1975, the homeowner would have spent around 30% of his or her monthly income on a house payment. In 2015, that same homeowner earning an average $4,300 a month would have to spend a little over 35% of his or her monthly income on a house payment. These figures also don't take into consideration the disproportionate cost increase of insurance, property taxes and general upkeep.

The result of the ever-widening chasm between income and prices has greatly decreased the net worth of most workers. This decrease has broadened the wealth gap, lowered the standard of living for most people and increased the amount of debt for masses. Most people are not trying to have more – well, not always. By and large, the problem results from trying to have what is needed to live. The problem becomes exasperated when a person justifies unnecessary purchases to minister to personal anxiety, to hide the truth from family, friends or social circles and/or are just too weak and financially ignorant to say no.

The recent economic challenges that came along with the Covid-19 pandemic has certainly made the situation more challenging for all but especially for Black people. There are no studies to prove this yet, but what little emergency savings Black people had has probably been wiped out. Money has probably been moved around from the priority of paying life insurance policies, investing and saving, to putting food on the table. We are the group of people that will always be at the highest end of the risk spectrum if we don't get our money situation under control.

Blacks Do Not Set The Culture For Money

One of Webster's Dictionary definitions for culture is the customary beliefs, social forms and material traits of a racial, religious or social group. Within America's culture are customary beliefs about money. For example, in America it is customary to believe that homeownership is part of the American dream since buying property is a great means to accumulate wealth.

Might I point out that the majority of what is considered American culture is basically White culture, with a few exceptions. That being said, if culture is defined as the customary beliefs of a people, the culture is not static but dynamic by default.

What is Black culture? Perhaps, it is a combination of what Blacks inherited from our African ancestors and what we have adopted, modified and learned throughout history. Our culture is a result of centuries of racial oppression and systemic under-resourcing. Such conditions have pushed us to be creative and industrious. From language to dress to scholarship...elements of Black culture are clearly distinctive and widely accepted by Black people. Our culture is not monolithic, it is a wide framework. It has been given credit as one of the major contributors to overall American culture.

Black culture can be seen in religion, language, family structure, food, music, dance, literature, art and so much more. It is about the community and the individual, giving back, the coolness and the drip, the spoken word and the written prose. Aspects of Black culture inform American life in a multitude of ways. Black culture is valuable. In fact, Black culture sets the trends for all other cultures in America including fashion, music, art and dance.

But therein lies the issue: Blacks do not set *the culture for money*. When American people think about wealth, money management, stewardship and financial knowledge, they don't think about Black people. In fact, Black people are the last group many of *us* think about when it comes to financial savvy or good stewardship.

Our culture is not just "hood"; it is Black excellence. Because of this, we must realign our financial focus from just "earning it to spend" to "earning it to grow more." If we are truly to be excellent, we need to adopt *the culture of money* more than any other people in America.

Why? There are laws and systems that disproportionately affect the Black community.

Something's got to give! We need to address the culture.

The critics blurt out the same narrative, which, no matter how you say it, purports that, "Black people don't know what to do with money." Many of our magazines and blogs point out the reasons why we need to educate ourselves. But our sub-economy can lift only if we buy into an ideology for wealth building. We are like ships without sails; some of us are blessed enough to land on a good island, but most of us

> We work more hours than any other racial group since the founding of this country and yet we have the least amount of wealth and the lowest per capita incomes.

get caught in winds and either drift or shipwreck.

We don't have the wrong culture of money, we have none at all! It's time we established one.

Money Impacts Everything

I cannot discuss money without talking about all the areas of our lives that money impacts. It can be legitimately included in the conversation about everything, but I'd like to address a few areas to convince you. Here's a non-exhaustive list of all the areas of our lives that money affects:

Health & Happiness – Money issues can cause stress, worry, unhealthy coping behaviors and injuries. Reports show that people who make less than $75,000 per household on average are less happy than those who make more. For people earning above $75,000 in annual income, there is a smaller correlation between money and happiness.

Productivity – Studies conclude that people who suffer from financial issues are less productive at work, at home and in their personal lives.

Relationships – Be real – it's hard to date when you're broke. Having financial resources allows us to enjoy a better lifestyle, have better access to our relationships and have the ability to do nice things for others.

Marriage – The leading cause of divorce and relationship strain is financial stress. I've done marriage counseling for over 20 years and I can tell you that more than a third of the cases that I have dealt with have to do with money issues and the stress created from poverty. Another issue that most couples don't discuss is the stress created from having two different views of money: one partner is frugal while the other is flashy. One wants to save while the other wants to spend. I've counseled so many couples who are near divorce simply because one partner had bad credit while the other had good credit.

Lifestyle – People miss out on life experiences and fail to reach goals due to the lack of health & wealth. While we work and receive a salary, how much we get paid affects our lifestyle, ability to save and ability to invest. It also affects how we live, where we live, how we vacation or if we can even *afford* a vacation.

Long-term Security – The lack of resources leads to the inability to afford important personal and financial goals such as retirement, financing our kids' college education and home or business ownership.

Business – Money affects entrepreneurship. You can't start a business unless you have capital. Even when talking about the personal goals of our life, like getting a better education – well, you need money. A college education costs as much as opening a business or buying a home in most regions. Those without resources have dreams that go to the grave with them, which negatively affects their well-being.

Technology – Tech isn't cheap. The latest iPhone costs

more than $1,000. That's the cost of a computer. In some respects, without money we're even locked out of the technological future that awaits us.

Investments – The reality is investing is based upon first having money. In other words, if you don't have any "extra money," then you will not have the ability to invest. It behooves you to understand everything you can about money and wealth (yes, there's a difference, which I'll point out later). We need to understand that living with margin creates excess. Saving and investing the excess, even a little, can become a lot over time. This is what reconstructionists knew. This is what grandma and grandpa knew – get an education, own something and pass it down. Why? Because wealth affects inheritance and legacy. It's great to pass down stories. It's great to pass down traditions. But it's even better to pass down those things along with some wealth.

Philanthropy – Of course, anyone who gives money away as a charitable act is practicing philanthropy, but you can't be a large donor philanthropist without an excess of money. Many people practice philanthropy from their wealth gained through investment activities or wealth-building activities like owning a business.

Faith – People develop a negative relationship with God, blaming him for their lack of provision in spite of their own poor stewardship. They don't practice generosity and tithing to the Lord's house as instructed, further alienating themselves from all God desires for them.

Community – Money affects our relationships beyond marriage. We talk about the solidarity of our community, but if we have no money in our community or churches, it's going to be difficult to finance and support the causes that improve our community. When you talk about community activism and solidarity, every activist needs money. Every church needs money to save souls. To march down the street with a sign, somebody's got to pay for the paper and the stick and the marker and in fact, to hire the lawyers to bail people out of jail. You need money to hire the lawyers to draft laws and opinions. We need money to host church services and put forth programs that improve the community.

Art – Money is a major theme found in some of the most important art that can be seen today. When the National Museum of African American History and Culture (NMAAHC) in Washington, D.C. first opened, it displayed a famous painting called *Redlined* on the third floor in the cultural community galleries. The painting's theme was about how Black people are redlined as the target of predatory lending practices. How much of rap and hip hop is about money? I imagine it must be well over 50% of the songs– having it, not having it or the lifestyle that money can afford.

Legal Rights – There are many people in our community that suffer from bad representation, no representation or underrepresentation simply because they can't afford the same-level lawyers as their White counterparts. Although OJ didn't have as many ties to our community as we would have liked before his infamous trial, we were excited to see him go free simply because he was a Black man who could afford the best lawyers.

There have been so many stories in our community where young Black men have been railroaded by laws—systems of oppression. They are innocent but considered guilty and they just could not afford a good lawyer. They had public defenders who were ill-equipped to face strong prosecution, as was the Central Park jogger case, which was all about money. Rich men like Donald Trump blasting and personally attacking young, poor Black men who are deemed guilty before being proven innocent. The Central Park Five didn't have the money or the support, nor did our community, to hire the type of lawyers that defended OJ. It took DNA evidence to overturn their convictions.

Leadership and politics – No matter what your political affiliation, Money and politics probably go hand in hand better than any other combination. Have you ever heard of the term super PAC? Technically known as independent expenditure-only committees, super PACs may raise unlimited sums of money from corporations, unions, associations and individuals, then spend unlimited sums to overtly advocate for or against political candidates. Unlike traditional PACs, super PACs are prohibited from donating money directly to political candidates.

Imagine if the Black community could create its super

PACs to lobby Washington D.C. politicians, on both sides of the aisle, to put forth bills and pass laws that would greatly affect our community. It wouldn't make a difference who was in office, Republican or Democrat, because we would have lobbyists working on our behalf. No, not Candice Owens – known for her pro-Trump activism and her criticism of Black Lives Matter and the Democratic Party – but brothers and sisters who would represent our interest and honestly care about our uplifting. But without wealth, we cannot accomplish this.

One of the largest super PACs in the country – Americans for Prosperity – is run by the Koch brothers. One cannot deny their political agenda as completely White American for the most part. Sure, there are ancillary benefits for all, but the language and the tone of their conservatism seems to have racial overtones.

Where are the Black Koch brothers? I don't know them, do you? That's why we need *the culture of money* because we need political influence. Let's just say, from the sacred to the secular, there is no area of our lives where money is not somehow involved. The whole conversation we're having today about the wealth gap is a fancy way of saying that Black and Hispanic people are born into more poverty than White people. It's a simple fact: there are people in this country who inherit more wealth than others within each generation. And the wealth that they transfer continually grows. That's why *we* need *the culture of money*.

Wealth, or the lack thereof, affects everything in our lives. If that's the case, we owe it to ourselves to develop and articulate an ideology, philosophy and theology of wealth. I would argue that understanding about wealth may be the civil rights issue of our day.

When you start to self-examine and make the behavioral changes necessary to realize the blessed life, you will want to *know more* about how to handle your money and pass down wealth to the next generation.

I am trying to shift you to want more for yourself, your family and your people. I am trying to shift you to do what is necessary to live and experience the blessed life. The Almighty has sent me as a messenger for this generation to encourage you to go get it and he has given me the blueprint for you to follow. I am *the culture of money*.

This isn't a gimmick for me. My testimony is bankrupt by 21, millionaire by 33! I've gone from being worth less than zero dollars to being able to accumulate wealth to pass down. My estate is considerable, and my grandchildren's futures are secured. *The culture of money* is not about "gaining the world and losing your soul," as scripture says. That's not profitable. It is all about a healthy wealth mentality.

Having wealth clearly won't buy you all the happiness in the world. Money won't make all your problems go away. But I can promise you that adopting *the culture of money* will solve a lot of your problems and bring you some happiness.

Our Money Subculture Needs Strengthening

As a people, we have gleaned and adopted principles about money but have yet to define our money subculture in a way that contributes to the overall American culture of money. For example, there is a clearly defined Jewish subculture of money—ideals and values passed down from generation to generation. The 2019 Jewish Museum London exhibition called "Jews, Money, Myth," explained one ideal with the following statement: "Money has symbolic as well as material value in Jewish life. According to Jewish customs, it is not a sin to be wealthy, but money must be used to serve God and to support the wider community."

Throughout the Bible, there are exhortations to give generously and be charitable. Consider the passage from Deuteronomy 15:11: *"There will always be poor people in the land. Therefore, I command you to be openhanded toward your fellow Israelites who are poor and needy in your land."* The possessive pronouns–the poor, the needy–suggest that it's an obligation of the heart for Jews to be generous.

Many of us outside the Jewish culture have encountered those ideals and values. Likewise, Asian Americans have a subculture of money that best reflects the values and ideals of their community. One of my Korean friends is married to a Chinese woman. He explained that even though Chinese and Korean cultures are vastly different, one of the values they both share in America is that investing in education is the primary goal for families. Education is worth money and children should be pushed to the highest paying fields to get the highest return on educational investment.

I'm not using these examples to trigger a "they are better than us" response. I'm pointing out that if culture is a set of customary beliefs, then we as members of the Black community should challenge ourselves to examine what we believe in respect to money. We need to articulate a position with the hope that we can pass something clear and profitable to the next generation.

We certainly have a culture of work. We've all been taught to work twice as hard to earn half the pay; to take great advantage of the opportunities we are offered; and to set the trend for others, especially when we are the "first" of our kind hired in a company.

Regardless of the media hot takes, there are millions of healthy and wealthy Black families. Yes, of course, the family structure has been broken down since the 1960s but we understand Black family culture, including generational messages we share such as, "You take care of your own"; "Don't put the family business in the street"; "Be your brother's keeper" and "Blood is thicker than water."

We have a strong church culture. Our worship is distinct; its sound is what others attempt to mimic. The term gospel music is synonymous with the Black church. We have such a strong and clearly defined church culture that there are millions of memes and hashtags that poke fun at Black church.

Just in case you doubt it, a recent Pew survey presents the case that three-quarters of Black Americans say religion is very important in their lives compared with smaller numbers of Hispanics (59%) and Whites (49%). Black Americans also are more likely to attend services at least once a week and to pray regularly. And 83% are more likely to say they believe in God with absolute certainty than Whites (61%) and Latinos (59%).[6] Why? Because our mommas made us get up and go to church. The funny thing is that even our most "thugged out" heathens know who Jesus is! They may not go to church but know, "We don't mess with Jesus!" We all know what church clothes are, even if the rules have been relaxed. Quiet reflection in the pews is not our way; we are expected to say "amen" and "hallelujah" as much as possible.

I could go on and on about clear distinctions and definitions of positive Black culture except for money and wealth. The closest I could get is when Lou Rawls used his platform to build the United Negro College Fund and taught us all to give back to HBCU's because "a mind is a terrible thing to waste." When it comes to our community, most discussions of money and wealth, even among ourselves, are all based in what Black people don't do! I'm tired of it and you should be, too. We can do better for sure. *The culture of money* shifts the conversation toward what Black people *will* do!

Sad, but true, our culture of money has been intentionally defined by the glorification of the "baller" or "balling." In fact, the phrase, "Wearing your wealth on your back," instantly brings to mind Black people. Why is this? What does this say about our culture of money? It says we need to define one, buy into it and *pass it down*. We can no longer afford to allow others to define us negatively regarding wealth and certainly, we cannot accept being negative toward ourselves.

We Need Money to *Future Proof* Black Culture!

Black culture is taking pride in who you are and where you come from. Who are we financially as a people? Where do we come from as a people? What has been handed down to us in terms of money culture? What was attempted to be handed down, practiced by ancestors, but rejected and presently lost?

Have we ever had a culture of money? Yes! The reconstruction period after the Civil War presents a clear culture of money. It is articulated best in the writings of W.E.B. Dubois who urged African descendants to educate themselves financially and otherwise. He urged them to own land and build enterprises and pass wealth down. He and his contemporaries may have worded it differently, but the principles of Reconstruction were to *know more, own more and pass down more.*

Dubois and others had a sense that the future of Black America relied upon the sacrifices of what was then their present Black America. To them, the view was longsighted. But something happened between then and now. Within certain Black families, there are clear money cultures, but as a whole community, we are not preaching, teaching, learning and modeling the most positive wealth behaviors we could be.

Black culture is progressive. We've gone from shackles to business ownership and making names for ourselves. By every statistical measure, we *own more* businesses than at any point in history and have broken more barriers than any previous generations combined. However, culturally, we don't place the highest value on the same things our ancestors did— knowing more, owning more and passing something down.

If we stuck with the plan the earliest freedmen developed in Reconstruction, we would be one of the wealthier racial groups. Instead, we embraced an American culture of excess at all costs, even though that leaves some of us with meager means. We've unintentionally embraced "showing" our worth versus actually "having" it.

To further develop the idea that culture is a set of beliefs passed down, I suggest that you cannot separate culture from values. A family's culture is developed from a family's values. Values are what guide us to act and behave a certain way. Therefore, the cultural values are not just things we hold true but a way of being and doing.

Three Values To Unify Us

First, we must aim to *know more*. Financial education is the cornerstone of financial freedom. Without it, Black people will suffer the financial fate of the types of emotional money management I discuss this in the next chapter. Beyond the emotions that keep us from having *the culture of money*, there is something else we need to call out: Ignorance. *"My people are destroyed from lack of knowledge,"* in Hosea 4:6 might be the best view of the results of ignorance–destruction. The wisdom in this verse points out that people will end up in financial ruin because they lack financial education. Since this verse is in the Bible, in context, we know that there are spiritual and relational consequences from this type of destruction. There is a clear and disclosed way that we are supposed to operate on the earth. Violate that protocol and destruction awaits.

I define ignorance as not knowing and being okay with not knowing. It's one thing to be unaware; we all have some things we don't know. It is another thing to feel okay with being muted or locked out. This is true ignorance. *The culture of money* is about always seeking to remove the boundaries of ignorance that cause destruction in our lives.

> Knowing more is a commitment to financial education. We cannot act on what we do not know, and what we do not know is killing us.

Financial education is the key to gaining our own financial breakthroughs. Gaining more knowledge is the first great investment you can make, and you don't need a lot of money to do so.

Invest in yourself to become educated, build skills and never be locked out again due to a lack of financial education. Value knowing and growing so that we are no longer left out of great economic booms or new wealth creation opportunities.

Once we *know more,* we can then seek to *own more.* Owning more is about serious wealth building. I need to pause here to share why these values are progressively important. Embracing one leads to the fulfillment of the next. In other words, you can't *own more* of the right kinds of assets unless you become financially educated. I perform financial healing workshops all over the country. In my post event surveys, the #1 personal finance topic people would like to learn more about is investing. While I commend those people for wanting to invest versus spend, I always urge them to consider the dangers of investing their hard-earned money while:

- Regularly carrying balances on high interest-rate credit cards
- Practicing inconsistent savings on a weekly or monthly basis
- Living without a budget that is tracked in a spreadsheet or personal finance app like Mint or Quicken
- Having an insufficient level of financial knowledge and confidence

They are putting the cart before the horse. Right idea but wrong order. The order is important. The quality of the assets you own is correlated to the quality of your financial education. Investing is not like the lottery. It requires a high level of financial education, patience to give money time to grow and consistent excess savings to invest regularly.

During the last decade, we have largely missed out on the greatest stock market run in history. In spite of the Covid-19 market correction of 2020, more wealth has been created in this market run than at any other point...but Black wealth creation during this market was not significant. Generally, most Blacks don't invest in the market; not because we can't or don't have access. There is a clear disconnect in what we know and understand about the market.

Owning more is embracing the mentality of our forefathers who left the plantations with one goal: to own their own land. This was best demonstrated in Alex Haley's book *Roots* when the whole family pooled their money together to buy land in Tennessee. The general consensus was that owning land was the way to solidify the family's Black identity and culture for future generations.

Even my grandparents, who may have missed the stock market, knew real estate was forced savings and equity they could leave to their children. When I was a child, almost every Black person I knew had grandparents who owned their home. Ownership is a mentality. God instructs the Israelites, *"To possess the land He has given them,"* (Numbers 33:53) because then and now, ownership allows legacy to happen. You can't pass down what you don't own. There is great value in owning homes, land, businesses, stocks, bonds, coins, art and all things that have appreciation potential over things that satisfy our personal wants.

We should invest in assets like our ancestors, did. They

aren't making more land anytime soon. To invest in equities, insurance and debt instruments that have historical wealth building appreciation, we must spend less on cars, oversized houses and designer brands...especially when we have non-designer budgets.

The culture of money values investing in opportunities like business ownership and venture funds. Presently, we do not have or we receive, few venture funds. We need to change that.

One Lifestyle to Identify Us

The central idea is to make moves today for a better tomorrow; to value long-term gain over short-term lifestyle gain. It is about investing today for an expected return tomorrow. It means we pursue thriving over surviving. It requires a commitment to understanding more about money and how it affects every aspect of life. It is a commitment to seeing yourself as an appreciable asset that requires consistent financial education investment.

The culture of money is not about instant gratification; making yourself feel good today only to live in financial pain for days, weeks, months and possibly years to come. We aim to have money and not just look like we have money. Instead, start thinking in the long term about every purchasing decision—what will buying this do for my tomorrow, not just my today? Ask yourself, is this purchase going to make me look good today and feel bad tomorrow? Thinking about your long-term need is the only way to create economic power. It is knowing that if you use money poorly today, it may destroy your tomorrow. Use money wisely today to predictably improve your tomorrow.

The culture of money is Jay-Z and Beyoncé. It is Fenty Beauty cosmetics brand by Rihanna. Looking at these wunderkinds, you see that making music can make you rich and investing in business can make you a billionaire. Supporting these types of companies, and their owners, is *the culture of money*. I will show you later, buying Black where and when you can will reward Black trailblazers with our purchasing power versus sowing success into companies that are tone deaf to our needs or might take advantage of our community.

The culture of money is...

- Instituting a financial plan, an estate plan, a retirement and living the good life
- Giving generously to our churches, social organizations and community groups
- Understanding the power of the individual, the family and the collective
- Amassing economic power to gain influence in the various realms of society
- Dealing ethically so we don't own enterprises and investments that destroy our own people
- Using our wealth to demand a political seat at the table

The Culture of Money Is Owning The Solution

Black excellence must be redefined to mean more than visual success defined by fit, title and lavish expenditures. We need to switch our focus to knowledge, wealth and legacy. We must own *the culture of money.*

One of the greatest compliments to the strength and excellence of Black culture is when the wider culture adapts our cultural norms as theirs. Imagine if our culture of money becomes the norm? I'm offering you a chance to become part of a movement. It takes just one person, who inspires one family, that changes one neighborhood, that uplifts one community, which then elevates one people.

The culture of money is future proof of Black excellence and taking it upon ourselves to *know more, own more and pass down more* to the next generation. Every Black church, educator, politician, corporate leader and family needs to own this. This is not my wealth movement: it's ours. I'm just the voice sent to provide navigation with an awakening message.

I expect you are receiving the progressive revelation – knowing more creates better ownership potential and owning more creates better legacy potential. *Passing down more* is simply leaving a financial inheritance and legacy values for the next generation. *The culture of money* just can't start and end with you. It is getting exhausting reading the stories about others who get a head start because of the birth lottery. They were just lucky enough to be born into the right family, living in the right zip code. This hurts because it implies being born Black is simply bad luck.

To change this, today's 20-year-old Blacks need to get woke about Black legacy. Today's 40-year-old Blacks need to become more self-sacrificing, so we have a future. Even if you don't accumulate the money to leave a financial legacy, make sure the next generation receives these Black cultural values to *know more*, *own more* and *pass down more*.

You must start right now. Today! As you begin to *know more*, start passing down knowledge and updated values so that your children will grow up with *the culture of money*.

The wealth gap is real. That tsunami is coming. The best way to tackle it will always be wealth generation for the purpose of leaving an inheritance.

> Every Black person, who can, should leave money. Every Black person must leave values.

As the Proverbs say, *"a good man"* or woman leaves an inheritance. This is a Black issue to solve. It is a major problem among Black people. We must own it individually and corporately.

TWO

You're A Slave to Money and Don't Know It

People need a breakthrough when they are stuck in the same behaviors and feel powerless to change them. Many have a public testimony to share about how well they are doing financially. We all have a shareable story, whether we open our mouths or not. The lifestyle someone *presents* speaks louder than the words he or she utters. These people mean well, but the picture they present is false. Like a phony Mona Lisa or a knockoff designer bag, it looks good, but it is fake.

The reason people do this is because they are too embarrassed and ashamed to admit what they don't know is killing them. Pride and ignorance are a dangerous combination. They need healing.

Let's Begin with A Proper Diagnosis

I have a friend who was eating dinner with his family one day and out of nowhere, he felt intense pain in his stomach. He said it was a pain like he'd never felt before and he couldn't eat one more bite. The pain continued for days. About a week later, he noticed his body was becoming fatigued much faster than it used to. He chalked it up to getting older. He continued to go to work every day and tried to live a normal life, but he couldn't because the pain kept getting worse. He decided to go to the doctor to get some tests run. One test led to another, but they all came back the same. He had prostate cancer. He was upset with himself and kept saying, "Why did I ignore the pain? I wish I had done something sooner, then I wouldn't be in such bad shape now!"

Sickness requires patients to be honest with themselves and admit they need a doctor instead of making themselves crazy with worry or trying to self-diagnose by searching the internet. They should seek out the help of a medical professional to conduct an exam to help discover the cause of the illness and develop a treatment plan to prevent the sickness from getting worse, so the body can heal. Healing requires maintenance and stewardship to prevent a repeat of the same illness.

Sickness doesn't just subside; it needs to be dealt with. Sickness needs a healer, divine or natural, but a healer, nonetheless. Financial illness is the same, whether it's caused by systematic oppression or poor personal stewardship.

My friend's physical pain and battle with cancer is a picture of how people deal with financial illness. The list of symptoms that manifest is long, including late payments, collection calls, bounced checks, maxed-out credit cards, repossessions, foreclosures, post-dating checks, stopping tithing, missed mortgage payments and so on. Yet, people ignore them. They also ignore their psychosomatic responses, like restless nights, increased anxiety, chest pains, constant worry, depression, migraines and so on. As humans, our natural inclination is to move away from pain and towards pleasure. It is why some avoid doctors. When these issues arise, people often continue to work and live their lives, with a wish and a prayer that their financial and bodily pain will subside.

This is an epidemic. People are financially ill when they:

- Have not clearly defined how much money they need to live the lifestyle they desire – whether now or in retirement
- Aren't even thinking about retirement – not thinking about it means they are either expecting to die young or live old and broke
- Don't want to face the future because it's stressful
- Think the future will automatically bless them no matter what they do with their money
- Avoid learning about financial health, especially when schools are not educating anyone on these matters
- Don't have a trusted financial mentor, adviser or money coach
- Lack financial knowledge and repeat the same negative behaviors
- Make poor financial choices because they don't understand their emotional drivers
- Lack confidence to make necessary financial moves

- Take financial advice from people trying to sell you something or friends who are living the lie themselves
- Expect unrealistic investment returns – like investing in bitcoin without enough money saved to survive the absolute collapse of the investment
- Continue to live with poor financial habits that developed at an early age with no idea how to live any differently

There is a plan working against people with no plan. Advertisers and retailers are ready to entice you to make a purchase today and forget about tomorrow. For example, when I was buying my first car at age 18, I was taken to the cleaners because I just didn't know the rules of the game. I accepted a high interest rate. I took advice from the wrong person; the one trying to sell me! We need to get advice from people who really can help us. If we ask the people close to us what *they* did, we may end up following them into the ditch. This starts at a young age.

Poor financial habits, lack of practical financial wisdom, compounding mistakes, low confidence, excessive credit card and student loan debt. Do any of these issues resonate with you? You cannot continue to avoid the elephant in the room. *You* may be the biggest reason that you are financially ill. Maybe it's not the devil, or the man, or anyone else; maybe you have contributed to this problem and only you can get you out of it.

It's Okay to Confess Your Faults

Start with step one. If you are financially ill today and your symptoms prove it, admit it. It's like being in Alcoholics Anonymous. The first step of deliverance is confession. You must admit, *"I am financially ill."* Jesus' brother James records in chapter 5:16 of his New Testament book that we are to "confess" our faults to each other. In that same verse, he concludes that doing so leads to healing.

Breakthroughs begin with confession. Don't be like my friend and let cancer grow in your body only to regret it later. This moment is for you. This is a different kind of altar call. It's actually a wake-up call in the spirit of Elijah for people who are financially ill to come to the altar and be healed. To come to the altar means to be ready to leave the past behind and receive what you need to move forward. It means to be healed, delivered and free. Every dream you have about your future, your heirs, your lifestyle and your achievements will die if you allow financial illness to continue to destroy your family from the inside out, just like cancer does.

There is no need to continue reading if you are not ready to confess. Why? You will view the revelations I'm sharing as merely information and you won't take action.

In the rest of this chapter, I'm going to share why people do what they do with money and move us further into financial healing so we can live *the culture of money.*

We Live the Financial Lie Because We Want To Impress Others

As mentioned previously, when it comes to financial illness, there are many people living that lie. They know they are sick, but they are too ashamed, embarrassed or afraid to deal with it. They hope and wish it would just go away. They testify about their money in what they drive, where they live, their position at work, how they vacation, where they hang out and how much they earn. But it's not real.

It's not bad to want to live your best life, travel well, wear designer items, live in a lovely home or drive a great car. It's only bad if the sickness is causing you to pursue those higher levels before your money can support them. Consider this – no one accuses Oprah of overspending even though she owns multiple mansions, employs chauffeurs, butlers and maids and wears red-bottom shoes like they are common flip-flops. The reason? Because with the amount of wealth she has accumulated, she can easily afford those items and her lifestyle. She is financially healed. She didn't even know how to use an ATM until a few years ago! She made the transition toward her wealth being a testimony that draws people and influences them.

This is what financial healing does; it makes our wealth part of, although not exclusively, the "salt" and "light" Jesus was speaking of in Matthew 5:13. There is nothing more contagious in a family, church or community than healing. No matter what type of healing it is, stories of healing inspire and increase the faith of the masses. Stars like Oprah, BET founder Robert Johnson or media mogul Cathy Hughes came from poverty. But through work, behavioral change and great faith, they rose above their meager beginnings. It is invigorating to behold. There is no way to count the thousands of people who've been inspired to pursue a greater life because of their testimony.

We live the financial lie because we want to impress others. I submit that it is the core basis for living a financial lie. We want people to think the best of us. We want our lives to speak well, to testify. Therefore, we should be able to understand the power of what a transformed life can do.

What If We Had the Balance Sheet to Back Up Our Testimony?

Think about what it will feel like to show a great life and actually *have* the wealth and means to back it up. Imagine being able to afford the bucket-list trip to Saint Tropez or Tahiti or stay at the 5-star hotel on Bora Bora and not damage your financial future. You *can* treat yourself to the finer things of life; just visualize them and make them part of your plan. That's right, you may have felt bad listening to cookie-cutter financial wisdom telling you not to splurge! That's a lie, too. You can splurge when you can *afford* to splurge. You don't need to be a billionaire like Oprah to splurge, but you must adopt the billionaire's mentality to wait for the right economic season to level up.

It's important that you dream, and you'll get no judgment

here. One person's dream can certainly differ from another's. You may want to own property to pass down to your children; your friend may want to drive a Bugatti; your momma might want to generously give to her church. As motivation, use whatever will inspire you to get financially healthier, to make the shift you need to make and not quit the process. My friend faced cancer and fought through the tough changes because he dreamed of being able to see his daughters get married. He said, "I'm going to go to every appointment, pray, eat well, exercise and laugh. I'll do whatever I need to do to beat this because I want to see them walk down the aisle."

What do you want to see? What is the testimony you claim that will be real? Let's agree, no more living the lie; embrace a new truth. God wants you to live the blessed life. He wants to bless you as much as you want to be blessed. He wants to bless you, going and coming, and everything your hand touches. He wants to fulfill in our people the promises he made a long time ago to Israel in Deuteronomy 28.

Black people have had to fight, scratch and claw for everything in this country, including basic civil rights. Outsiders and those in our community who want to play it safe will accuse me of encouraging a victim mentality. I told you in the beginning, this book is not safe. *The culture of money* is not safe. It is for Black people who seriously want to radically reduce the wealth gap by *knowing more, owning more and passing down more*. We claim our financial healing because we confess our fault. We build a safe space for Black people to be financially healed. We bring this ideology into our institutions so we can continue the process. We will not apologize or explain to anyone about why we have the best things life has to offer. We dream. We go get it.

We will no longer show and live a lie. We will be "salt" and "light" and allow our financial healing to inspire others. We will not testify about our money, but with God's strength, we will make our money testify. Now, let's go to work!

Financial Healing Requires Identification of Emotional Bondage

To receive financial healing, we need to identify our negative financial behaviors and work to break their stronghold. Every financial activity has an emotion associated with it. I call these "money-motions." We need to examine what happens with our emotions as we experience financial transactions and activities. Part of the reason we've lived the financial lie is because of unchecked and unexamined money-motions.

Let's examine my money-motions for a second. I filed bankruptcy at age twenty-one simply because I was trying to prove that I made it out of the hood and was doing better. I wanted people to see a young Black man making it. Was there anything wrong with me feeling that way? Absolutely not! I think most people who came from a similar background would agree. Why shouldn't I want people to see me doing well when most of my life was financially challenging, like most other Black people? I felt proud. We often give pride a negative connotation, but there are also good forms of pride.

If you are proud of your church or your family, there's nothing wrong with that.

The issue is when money-motions aren't examined, managed and checked, something good can become something bad. Unchecked pride can be a warning sign of a fall. My pride was unchecked, so it led me to spend money to fulfill that money-motion. I was proud that I had a good job and was making a little money. I spent most of that money to feed my sense of pride. Do you see the deception? It was fine for me to be a proud Black man, making it in a completely White space. Yet, it was not right for me to feed that money-motion by spending to prove to others that they should put respect on my name.

Emotions affect how we use money, which in turn affects our ability to build wealth and execute our long-term financial plans. At twenty-one, pride drove me to bankruptcy court.

Unpacking the "why" behind what we do is critical to the healing process. Failing to examine how we got financially ill and the money-motions that played a part is like telling a doctor you have a lump on your chest, but he does not test you for cancer.

Psychologist Robert Plutchik's wheel of emotions theory offers eight emotions that need to be understood regarding money: fear, anger, sadness, joy, disgust, trust, anticipation and surprise. To one degree or another, all these emotions apply to our financial decisions. Money is tied to almost all of our psychological needs and resulting behaviors, including my additions to the list, which include greed, false hope, wishes, embarrassment and shame.

Your Money and Emotions Are in a Potentially Disastrous Relationship

It's a generally accepted rule that relationships work best when two parties mutually benefit each other. The worst relationships are those where one party does not reciprocate or takes advantage of the other.

Relationships can be complicated. People spend a lot of time searching on the Internet, consuming content that can help them become better at relationships. Yet, every person is in a relationship with their own money. In fact, most people are in a very toxic relationship with their money.

Excellent relationships operate smoothly and allow you to appreciate your own life, work and actions. You are not always worrying or speaking about it. Just like an auto that is running smoothly, you do not need to keep fixing it. This is a picture of you and money in a good relationship. You will be able to appreciate your life, work and what they allow you to experience. When you and money are running smoothly, you don't need to keep talking and worrying about it.

Automobiles require upkeep. Pay attention to them and they work better. Money works the same way. You probably spend more time talking and worrying about your money than anything else outside of family. Since you spend so much time with your money, you need to master this relationship.

How well do you study this relationship? Is your money and emotion relationship healthy or unhealthy? Can you connect habits like spending, saving or investments to emotional drivers? A money and emotional relationship can make you very happy or unhappy, so understanding emotional drivers is an important part of moving toward healing. If the relationship isn't working, changes have to be made.

No matter what you've done in the past, as a financially healed person, it's up to you to find out how to avoid a similar bad relationship in the future. Examine yourself. Failure to understand what money-motion caused your last spending spree, which resulted in a late rent or mortgage payment, will cause you to repeat those negative behaviors.

As a financially healed person, it is critical to identify your own money-motions and create a long-term plan for your finances in order to experience behavioral change. It's time to understand how negative money-motions such as fear, greed, shame and embarrassment have influenced past financial decisions, and contributed to your current financial status. This will help you see the more positive money-motions and cycles that can move you toward financial health. Let's dig deeper.

Mastering Money-Motions Will Shift Your Financial Behaviors

Did you know that studies prove your financial decisions are based primarily upon emotions and not logic? If you disagree, I'll explain my theory.

Most likely the last designer item you purchased was 100% emotional, not logical. It doesn't matter how much you spent, whether it was $300 for a belt or $3,000 for a purse. Walmart, Target and Marshalls all sell belts and purses for less than $20. All belts hold up pants and complement the same-colored shoes. In other words, a black belt will do the job as long as it is black and holds up your pants. My wife loves shoes and purses. She moves her same old stuff from one purse to another. It's never new stuff that the old purse can't hold. My point is that all purses do the same thing. Likewise, unless my body shape changes drastically, any new belt I buy will do the same thing the last belt did.

But let's be honest. Most times when you walk pass the window of Ferragamo, Givenchy, Fendi, Gucci or Louis Vuitton, all logic fails because you are emotionally attracted to their designs and value as status symbols. You may see yourself and your fit at the next level. You may visualize and "feel" something, whether it's pride, joy, excitement or a litany of other emotions that drives you to make that purchase. I can promise you that the item you purchased was not "needed." You didn't purchase the belt or bag because you had a logical reason. It was because of how it would make you feel to own and wear it. The purchase had nothing to do with utility, need or function.

Meanwhile, back at the ranch, the "millionaire next door" strides into Walmart to buy a basic black belt, then invests the rest of her money in the purchase of a company or stocks. She is driven by wealth logic while you are taken by money emotion.

The culture of money is embracing wealth logic over

money-motions. People who live outside *the culture of money* often succumb to impulse purchases because they are not aware of their money-motions. Let's face it, emotions are volatile and often can't be trusted, so why trust your emotions when spending your hard-earned cash?

Almost nothing can be more of an emotional rollercoaster than your daily money dealing. Right now, you are either making money or losing it.

Detach your emotions from your money and you will make better financial decisions. You may think money is serving you, but perhaps you are serving your money. It could be your master. And guess what? Your emotions

> Everything you pay for today—your rent, mortgage or car—is either moving you toward or away from your long-term financial goals.

are at the root of the deception.[1] Most people go through life thinking of their experiences as isolated, unrelated events, but in fact every experience we have is an opportunity for learning. In order to learn from our experiences, we need to link them together and construct meaning from them. That process requires reflection.

Reflection is a Biblically endorsed activity. Proverbs 8:12 associates it with wisdom: *"I, wisdom, dwell [with] prudence and find the knowledge [which cometh] of reflection"* (Darby). Other Bible translations present the idea that this wisdom provides foresight: *"I, Wisdom, live with insight and I acquire knowledge and foresight"* (God's Word). Therefore, reflection involves linking an experience to things we have previously learned. In education circles, this is known as scaffolding. As we reflect, we draw cognitive and emotional information from all our sensory sources: sight, hearing, smell, touch, taste and feelings.

When you reflect, take time to look back before moving forward. This is how foresight develops. Take a break from what you're doing, step away from your spending and ask yourself, "What have I learned from this experience?"

When you reflect on past financial experiences and what you learned from them, there is no way to "fail" or "make a mistake" in the normal sense of those terms. Rather, by visualizing what you experienced and reflecting on what each part of the experience meant, you'll gain personal insight that allows you to learn from all of your financial experiences.[2] According to the Proverbs, this is wisdom. It is unwise to continue what you are doing without reflection. It's time to reflect on a few money-motions that might be driving your fiscal management.

Fear and Greed Are Powerful Drivers

Fear and greed are powerful emotional drivers: politicians and the investment community surely know it. Often, politicians use high-contrast fear mongering to drive voters to the polls. "Vote for me because I will save you from the Mexicans trying to cross the border to kill innocent Americans!" a Republican proclaims. This works sometimes because many White people are afraid of violence spilling over into their neighborhoods; especially potentially violent Brown people! Ironically, it's the Brown people who should fear for their lives since the most unpunished crimes in the history of America are hate crimes, lynching and terrorism against Brown-skinned people.

Greed works equally well as an emotional driver, especially with high-risk investment schemes. Have you been to a real-estate seminar lately? They all sound the same. A video opens showing a montage of the speaker's lavish lifestyle, subliminally sending the message that you are living beneath your privilege and you could have all of this. The speaker coos, "Don't you want to live like me?" At the end of the video, the presenters try to sell you a kit for $1,000, $5,000, $10,000 or whatever the market will bear to learn the secrets of their success.

Millions of dollars are being made from the desire of every man to have it all, which is a nice way of saying "greed." Americans are prone toward greed: it is a functional necessity of capitalism. Adam Smith, an 18th century political economist and some say the father of capitalism, said that greed drives the market and makes us "self-maximizing" individuals.

When it comes to money, greed is what causes people who are doing well financially to keep raising the bar. It is what causes people to begin to count their profits before they are realized. Greed is what drives market bubbles. People believe real estate will keep appreciating without interruption and so they buy more to cash in on the boom. They believe the stock market will never have a correction; the bull runs, so they keep buying, especially high-risk IPOs and bitcoin, to get rich or richer. This is all based on the emotion of greed.

Fear works the opposite way. This emotion drives people to retract hard when things start going south because they don't want to lose everything. Worry causes people to avoid making decisions out of fear that they will make the wrong choice. Fear is also based on lack of knowledge, which breeds low confidence, which then develops into what is called the "fear freeze."

When people lack confidence and knowledge to make financial decisions at difficult times, most freeze up. During the Covid-19 Pandemic in 2020, the fear freeze gripped our country. It caused many people to spend only for basic necessities like housing, food and yes, the INTERNET! For once, lavish travel and designer fixings were not the highest priority. Out of this chaos, great investment and business opportunities were created, but most individuals missed them because of their fear freeze. They feared making another wrong decision. Consider how *the freeze* might affect these situations:

- If a child has a bad experience with letting a friend borrow something, she might grow up afraid to share, give or take any risk
- If a college-bound student is overwhelmed by student loan documents, he may just sign them without understanding. The fear of seeming stupid causes anxiety and leads to a bad decision

- If a married couple selects a *bad* mortgage solution, it won't be long before they are in a financial bind and possibly a few months away from losing their home. Later in life, this couple may shy away from purchasing a new home because of their early difficulties with a mortgage, possibly locking themselves out of the real estate market

Fear and greed drive most of our financial decisions!

False Hope, Luck and Wishing Are Black Kryptonite

On the other end of the spectrum are the emotions of false hope, luck and wishing. State governments have used lotteries to fatten their budgets to the demise of many needy individuals. The lottery is designed to take full advantage of false hope, luck and wishing money-motions.

Growing up, I watched so many unsuspecting and uninformed people religiously play the lottery daily with their meager take-home pay. Their money-motions blinded them from the truth. If they saved that money daily from every check, they would have some savings to fall back on. Furthermore, if they invested what they saved, they would hit the same lottery that the wealthy hit on consistently – the long-term gains available in the stock market.

Why do people waste money on the lottery? Mainly because of false hope and wishing. They falsely hope they will hit the big one. Then they wish all their financial troubles would go away with one lucky draw, scratch off or pull of the lever. These two money-motions tie very closely to luck.

Potential good fortune drives a lot of people to play slot machines all night long at the casino. This thought pattern is dangerous because it gives

> We wish for good luck because it doesn't require obedience to anything or anyone.[3]

people a false sense of confidence that if they are in a financial bind, they just have to wait until their ship comes sailing in like the last time they won big. They might have felt lucky when they scratched off and won $100 (even though they spent thousands of dollars over the years). The problem is that luck, like false hoping and wishing, can cause people to think that they can continue to make the same bad decisions and get the same results. Why else would you spend thousands to win one hundred dollars? False hoping and wishing drive you to chase after the one lucky scratch-off, lever pull or magic number to change your financial future.

Luck is a terrible desire. It will cause people to get greedy, because they often think that whatever they did worked out the last time, even though their decisions violated clear financial wisdom.[4]

Here's an example: a man overspends on his family vacation but returns to work and receives an unexpected bonus check. If he trusts in luck, he may believe that he can and should repeat his overspending behavior again and again. Instead of budgeting and planning for the family's next vacation, he wings it and upgrades the hotel room anticipating that some extra money may come his way with enough time before the credit card bill comes due. The problem is that company bonuses, like company earnings, are not as predictable as his bad decision making. He will most likely receive a credit card bill he can't afford and end up in bondage to a credit card company. Visa becomes his boss because luck fooled him. You can't build a fortune going to Vegas and getting lucky because the house always wins. Luck is not to be trusted.

On the other hand, the same false hope and wishing money-motions often drive entrepreneurs to start businesses because they want to carve their own path, control their own destiny and wish to make millions. I've launched and shuttered more than a few businesses, and every idea I had seemed like the "million-dollar" idea. Why? False hope and wishing.

That's the problem with undiagnosed false hope and wishing: they often cause individuals to inflate the potential for outcomes and returns, leading them to make bad investments, succumb to pyramid schemes, waste money on gambling, invest in a bad idea or send money to a televangelist in exchange for a miracle cloth. Check out these quotes:

- *40% of Americans are counting on the lottery, sweepstakes, marriage or an inheritance to fund their retirement.* – Walter Updegrave, Senior Editor of *Money Magazine*. This will not change your family's future. It's not you taking control of your life and doing the hard work

- *When past bubbles burst (real estate, stock market), people relied on 'hoping' the markets would turn around and ignored obvious signals.* There are always clear signs of markets turning yet people stay in hoping it will turn around. Be prepared and prepare yourself mentally for making tough decisions

- *[There are] signs of froth in some local markets where home prices seem to have risen to unsustainable levels. –* Alan Greenspan

- *As the bubbles formed, people didn't want to 'miss out.'* – Warren Buffett

Buffett didn't invest in tech and stayed in his comfort zone. People teased him about missing out on the next greatest thing. Yet staying true to its roots, his company Berkshire Hathaway has maintained its values in spite of market downturns because Buffett doesn't let false hope and wishing take advantage of him. He knows what he understands and will not invest in what he doesn't.

Certainly, being hopeful can be a positive. One of my favorite passages in the Bible is Romans 5:1-5, but particularly the way verse five ends *"hope will not disappoint."* The verse speaks to how faith justifies us and allows us to face insurmountable odds and situations. It builds upon the premise that hard times build perseverance and perseverance builds character. Once character is developed, hope is also justified. It's a gift resulting from the love of God being poured into our hearts. Yes, hope can be a driving emotion fully based in faith and supported by strong character. This is the kind of hope that actually works in our favor to guide us to making the right decision and proper dreaming.

Most people don't take time to learn and study their money-motions. Most are not confident because they are not well-educated and prepared in these matters. You must have hope. But false hope not based in logical action is not profitable. It's good to have personal dreams and goals, but you must do something with them. There are specific actions that get specific results. Hoping can work as long as it doesn't violate the rules of financial logic.

Almost everyone reading this book probably has hoped or wished that they will become a millionaire someday (if they haven't already). Becoming a millionaire is easy. One way: start in your 20s and consistently invest $100 a month wisely. That idea is not far-fetched. Unfortunately, you can't just wish $1 million into existence. But if you are consistent, disciplined and faithful to financial principles then you *will* be able to build your wealth. Yes, it's that easy.

Shame and Embarrassment Are Black Shackles

The singing duo Mary, Mary told us all to take the shackles off our feet so we can dance. Shame and embarrassment are the shackles that hurt Black people in more ways than I can count. Embracing these emotions will cause you to ask fewer questions, pretend to be and know too much and end with your financial ruin.

Most people won't change their financial behaviors, even though they are financially ill and know it, because they don't want to face down shame and embarrassment. There is one who pretends to be rich, but has nothing; another pretends to be poor, but has great wealth.[5]

I'll call it like I lived it. While fear and greed are big emotional drivers, shame and embarrassment can't be overlooked. People don't want to deal with the pain of shame and embarrassment. The reason it's so hard for people to come to grips with these money-motions is they've probably built up the public perception that they are doing better financially than they really are. They are living a lie.

It doesn't matter whether they are earning $20,000 or $100,000 a year, the public persona created is that they are living their best life but privately, they are struggling, evidenced by their late payment on monthly bills. Shame and embarrassment are two of the most deceptive money-motions destroying the good plans God has for us and we need to gain victory over them.

The data says most Americans don't know as much about money as they post on social media. Most aren't as fiscally disciplined as they pretended to be. We needed a Pandemic to finally pay attention to the truth – we live with little margin! What would happen if the world found out that you were late on the Mercedes-Benz payment last month? Or that you went to Louis Vuitton and bought that incredible designer item, only to be begging your cousin for rent money two months later? What if the world knew that you have been working for 10 years at a corporate job, but you have very little savings because you rarely invest? Maybe you haven't saved because your Big Spender money personality caused you to prioritize traveling five-star during the summers instead of building wealth. While some of your coworkers are bragging about how their investments have grown to nearly $500,000, you're sitting there with less than $5,000 in the bank. All these are embarrassing situations.

When I conduct workshops, it's inevitable that some people in the room, because of shame and embarrassment, will pretend that they know everything I'm teaching. There will be another group who feels that teaching basic financial principles is too basic for them. They will always come up to me afterward and state how they were hoping for something more because of the "level" they are on. Then I'll investigate the strength of their margin (savings and investments) and find out they want to know how to invest in private equity with piggy bank money. Why? They are too ashamed to admit that they are not the smartest financial people in the room, especially in front of those to whom they have bragged, flaunted lifestyle and their "level." Shame and embarrassment will cause you to miss what you don't know because you are too busy promoting what you *think* you know.

Facing down shame and embarrassment requires change, but most people are uncomfortable with change, so they ride out the lie. When shame and embarrassment are combined with false hope and wishing, people begin to think their fortunes will change eventually with some stroke of luck, or if they are religious, with blessings. This leads many of them to stay stuck, even though they are miserable.

Being miserable can also feel safe. This is what I call the "Financial Patty Hearst Syndrome (FPHS)." It's the result of shame and embarrassment gone unchecked. It's when a person is taken captive by these two money-motions. Instead of trying to leave captivity, they somehow grow an affection for poverty, for lack and for private struggle. Why? Because financial struggle is familiar; it's all they know. And while they may be struggling, at least they know that space well. They are complacent in the acceptance that perhaps this is all there is.

People with FPHS also fear what life would look like if they were free. They don't want to face the pain of exposing themselves to the world saying, "Financially, I'm not fit." They're ashamed that they are out of shape, their budgets aren't chiseled or that they are actually financial wrecks.

Rather than deal with their shame and embarrassment, they'd rather go down, as 50 Cent said, *"Die tryin'"*; suffering through a slow financial death in a smoldering pile of debt and poverty.

Ask yourself this... "Why am I trying to impress a bunch of people that don't really care about my financial future?" The people you *think* you need to impress don't care if:

- Your kids might inherit nothing
- The next generation of your family might live perpetually broke
- You may never get to retire because you put no money aside for the golden years
- You may never get to move out of your apartment into a home
- You get evicted or foreclosed on because you spend all your money trying to keep up with the Joneses

They don't care! So why do you care so much about them? Why are you trying to impress people you don't know and who don't really know you? Do you hear yourself saying, "I want to show them I've arrived?" I'll ask you again…why are you trying to impress them with fancy cars, three-car garages or a luxury apartment (especially if you can't afford them)? They don't care that you've arrived. And it's not going to change how they feel about you. The only thing they're going to do is be in the crowd laughing when you lose it all. Because that's what "they" always do. They'll celebrate you while you're on top, but they'll certainly abandon you when you're on the bottom. It's been this way for thousands of years.

Will the people you're trying to impress come when you call to help you out of a tight spot? Will they help you with your mortgage payment on your too-big house? The answer will most likely be "no" or "sorry, I can't possibly spare it." Even worse, they may put your business out in the street or gossip and laugh when your financial lie is revealed, saying, "Look at them, they thought they were all that; they thought they had money and they're broke." Ha, Ha.

Understand that shame and embarrassment are money emotions keeping many of our community in lack. Today is a good day to hold a funeral for all the negative money-motions that are holding us back from prosperity. God made you to impress him, so stop trying so hard to impress everybody else. Get the healing you need in every area of your life, including your finances.

THREE

Why $1,000,000 Right Now Will Destroy You

We have already unpacked how *money-motions* influence your financial habits, now let's focus on how your attitudes and values related to money also influence and shape your financial habits. Values and attitudes are so inseparable that I call them *money scripts*. Before, I further define money scripts, let's lay a foundational understanding that our values and attitudes work together.

Values are those things that we believe. Attitudes are how we feel about something based upon those values. For example, people who believe that Black contractors do inferior work are usually raised with a value system that promotes the inferiority of Black contractors. As a result, their attitude and behaviors toward Black contractors will be negative. They develop habits in dealing with Black contractors based upon their values, attitudes and emotions. Values are intrinsically passed down or intentionally adopted. They are based on how we were raised or that to which we were exposed. As we age, we begin to question how we were raised. Some values we modify, some we keep and then we intentionally adopt and incorporate new values. Prior to doing that, we were operating with whatever values were passed down to us.

Therefore, your money attitudes are based upon your values. These values and attitudes compose *money scripts* which auto play every time you make financial decisions.

The National Financial Educators Council (NFEC) research shows that our childhood experiences shape us as we transition into adulthood and into people that develop "money scripts." The NFEC model describes four main "money scripts": Money Avoidance, Money Worship, Money Status and Money Vigilance. I have added a fifth and very important script that often plays out in the minds of Black people. It's based upon our unique American experience: Money Reparations. People develop one of these scripts which auto plays, and becomes the predominant attitude which most influences their financial behaviors.

Here are the five money scripts:

- **Money Avoidance.** People who follow this script believe money is bad and/or they don't deserve money. To these people, money is scary. They believe money "changes people" and "it's the root of all evil."

- **Money Worship.** These people believe money will solve all their problems, and there will never be enough. To them, money brings power and happiness. They are prone to be part of the hustle culture. They are most vulnerable to get-rich-quick schemes and prone to believe, "If I hit the lottery I will...." To them, every problem sounds like a money one.

- **Money Status.** People in this category believe that owning the newest and best possessions conveys status. These are the Gucci saints! Having nice stuff is a safe space and there can never be too much of it.

- **Money Vigilance.** Vigilant people embrace frugality, recognize the importance of saving and tend to keep quiet about how much money they have or make. They often believe in frugality and "don't let people know what you have." Think of the old Black guy who turns his back when he counts his money.

- **Money Reparations.** These people believe money ministers to their past wounds, it heals, and its primary purpose is reparations for past injustices. They feel, no matter what, they deserve to have it because of what they've been through. I added this category to the NFEC's model because it might be the #1 script secretly playing in the minds of Black people.

The foundation for financial healing is to identify the

emotions that are influencing your money habits. The next step is to identify what money scripts trigger you to make poor financial decisions.

If you are not reaching your financial goals, first your money-motions and second, your money script may indicate what's holding you back from financial healing. Every person has money scripts, so there's nothing inherently wrong with them, but what you don't know about them might be killing you. Without awareness and management, these scripts will get out of control.

When the Money Reparations script auto plays, you justify poor financial habits because your attitude is you deserve something. You will treat yourself! It becomes a means of self-therapy, self-ministry and catharsis. The Money Reparations script doesn't necessarily clamor for luxuries like Money Status—they feel like they are owed anything they want–it's an internal cry for 40 acres and a mule. It could be something as simple as an ice cream cone. You may not have the extra $5 for an ice cream, but on a hot summer day you will hear the script in your head say, "After all you've been through and all the racism you experienced, you deserve this ice cream!" And you will buy that ice cream because the Money Reparations script says that somebody owes you something and thus you've got to take it upon yourself to treat yourself. I give restitution to myself for the wrongs done to me. And I believe this one may be the most deceptive and the most dangerous one. For Black people you could argue this super script may also influence some of the other scripts.

If you combine the Money Reparations script with the Money Status script, it makes it even more dangerous.

Likewise, people who have the attitude of Money Avoidance will never reach their full earning potential by asking for promotions and raises. For them, money is scary. Money doesn't really offer pleasure, having it leads to pain. Because money is a foe, money can never be a friend.

Money Worship will cause you to focus so much on leveling up your life with success that you might make a wreck of your relationships. The obsession with a "love of money" might lead you to poor habits.

Money Status people live on credit, but they look good. This script is what caused me to end up in bankruptcy. As a young corporate professional, I wanted to prove to "them" that I was on their level and belonged. I bought the watches, cars and clothes to show I was "from the hood but not of the hood!" Money Status people are prone to having too much house, a big apartment, nice cars, name brands and everything else they can't really afford.

For those who lean toward Money Vigilance, like my wife, Terri, on the surface all seems well because they might save and invest more but they need to be aware of tendencies to be overly restrictive and avoid risks they could take, such as investing in real estate, starting a business or investing in the stock market.

In *The Culture of Money* workshops, we help participants identify their money script. Remember, identification of your money-motions is the first step of financial healing but the second step is identifying and managing your money script.

Since money is emotionally driven, more than it is logical and rational, the objective of identifying your money-motions and script is self-awareness. There can be no change without truth. Only truth makes us free![1] Truth provides us emotional intelligence and space for healing. The goal is to look at your money habits objectively and discover where you are challenged.

We all default to a money script based upon how we were raised, and what we were exposed to. Our values can either be inherited or adopted. Based upon those values, certain scripts play. Advertisers often attempt to rewrite our script and give us new ones to embrace. The default script that advertisers want us to succumb to is "money is status," and by having it and buying the best things, we should feel good about ourselves.

When it comes down to the entrepreneurial world selling us, the default status is "money will solve all your problems" (in other words – money worship). So, the financial world wants you to default to the idea that money will solve all your problems, and the consumer product world wants you to default to money is status.

Money Status Is the Default Script for Advertisers

Financial psychology is a somewhat overlooked but growing space between general psychology and behavioral economics. It is a much-needed subject to review since advertisers and marketers study this space. Consumers should do the same.

Let's dive deeper to understand what is happening to us in the marketplace. By the time we reach age 18, we have seen at least one million sales messages. Commercial entities have busted budgets to manipulate consumers. The dirty little secret is to make consumers feel insecure about their social status and personal happiness – to appeal to the need for status. The ads are created with psychology in mind, to subliminally make us think we would be less successful and unhappy if we miss out on the latest "thing."

We are exposed to more messages to buy stuff than we are to save and invest money. Targeted ads are making it more difficult to avoid buying on the Internet. We are bombarded, and our emotions are constantly triggered. The more wireless the world gets, the more we are at the mercy of sophisticated algorithms triggering us to buy. Social media was created for one reason; not to bring us together for kumbaya, but to bring us together to buy stuff. You see more product ads now than when Instagram first started, but that was always part of the monetization plan. Social influencers push Money Status. They have joined in to tell us we are not living our best life, so we feel bad, get triggered and try to make ourselves feel better with buying, even if we destroy our financial future by doing so.

Online shopping alone has changed money behaviors. Over the past 20 years, we have experienced more extreme spending than ever before. The goal for advertisers is to get people to spend and do it impulsively. The advertisers are colluding to trigger one dominant money script: Money

Status. They want us all to feel like having "the best" and "most expensive" should be our aim. We are driven to be *impulsive spenders*. It is not enough to have a button that says *BUY* – it must say *BUY NOW*. Buying is not their only goal, but to do it *NOW*. Everything is driving us to make irrational, illogical, and emotional financial decisions that result in poor stewardship.

Our impulses are being triggered with every swipe and click to get that thing we feel like we're missing – the thing that gives status, something to talk about, or make us unique in our friend circles. They are taking full advantage of our money scripts.

Looking back twenty years, having to go to brick and mortar stores was more inconvenient. Today every deal in the world is right on your computer screen or smartphone. The plan for the Internet was always to sell, sell, sell, just as its television and radio advertising predecessors. Even "free information" has a cost to it; providing your email. Savvy marketers know how to hook people online, like unsuspecting fish, and throw a little free bait to entice us into a sales funnel for a purchase later.

I know many people who have taken the bait, hook, line and sinker. I have myself on many occasions. Yes, I allowed the marketplace to sell me things I did not need, all while struggling to make car and housing payments on time within thirty days of the unnecessary purchase. I wasn't alone; this is the illness many are suffering from today.

Let's be honest, we are very emotional people. There is no

killing our passion. You see our passion when we preach and do spoken word. No one else sings with our emotion. It's called soul. Everything we've survived comes bubbling up in our own unique way of being and doing. We call it Blackness. Others misinterpret this and see it as hostile, but it's not. It's beautiful, it's Black, it's us, so just accept it.

While our emotion is strong, it can also work against us. It can make us most vulnerable to Money Reparations or Money Status scripts causing us to impulse spend even more when we might have even less. It just isn't fair. Don't you think they know that if people have been disenfranchised and feel generally unappreciated, they may need to feel the best about themselves? That they may offer themselves reparations? That they may want to have status and feel great? So, the marketplace says, "I have a solution for you. You can escape the world where you are less than by becoming socially more acceptable by buying this. Don't you want the Lexus delivered to the house for Christmas with the big bow on it? Won't you feel good about yourself if you wear this nice outfit or stay in this upscale hotel?" And we subconsciously scream, "Yes, Lord," from deep inside.

We need to better understand how this more efficient purchasing environment affects us, so we better control our hard-earned dollars instead of letting our dollars be controlled by a third-party vendor. Understanding this will help us become more rational and savvy people less prone to schemes and less impulsive.

Trey, the Classic, Clueless Victim

I suggest that if anybody ought to be aware of how advertisers are taking advantage of consumers, it's us. With the wealth gap that exists, we *literally* cannot afford to keep getting played by the marketplace and driven to the impulsive money personality type. Our money needs to go into ownership of appreciable assets that we can bequeath versus stuff we will eventually donate to Goodwill or throw away.

I have a friend named Trey who is a college-educated, mid-level executive in the tech industry. He's married with three kids and lived in a nice three-bedroom home in the suburbs. He had two cars, a Mercedes E-Class and a Lexus SUV for his wife. Their combined yearly household income was $160,000. Surprisingly, his home was foreclosed on a few years ago. Now you may ask, "How could that be possible?" Many things caused the default, but one that cannot be ignored is the emotions that caused him to overspend. His financial illness destroyed him from the inside like a cancer. He did not have *the culture of money*. By his own admission, he bought stuff that made him feel great and like he had made it versus visualizing his future, making a financial plan and working the plan with the gifts God had given him.

With little to no savings to fall back on after he lost his job, he had to move out of the house where his kids were born and raised. It was a very emotional day. He described his feelings of failure, shame and embarrassment. He said he was very angry with himself, and kept reliving and replaying in his mind all the opportunities he had to manage his money differently. What he regretted most was spending the household's $160,000 combined income to level up his lifestyle versus setting up a great and more relaxing future. He admitted that with all that money rolling in, it felt like he was making up for all the things he could not get and all the places he could not go. Bringing in six figures made him feel like he could do whatever he wanted. All the emotional descriptors in Trey's story, both positive and negative feelings, were tied to money.

I didn't know Trey was struggling with financial illness until he had to move out of his house. He said he never told me because he was too embarrassed. I went to help Trey on moving day. I promised to help him get back on his feet now that I knew he was struggling. He was wearing a Gucci striped belt, 7 Mankind jeans and an Off-White t-shirt. Yes, he used to be a hype beast. His wife packed up the house with her Louis Vuitton bag on the counter. I was sad. I couldn't help but think that they had spent at least $4,000 on the items I just mentioned. Between them, the cost of their apparel added up to at least two mortgage payments. I couldn't help but think they might have been able to stay in their home if they had played this all differently.

A few weeks later I invited Trey to grab coffee. I wanted to understand how a family that earned so much money could end up with a house in foreclosure. They had spent money on things that made them feel good in the moment, but hurt their financial future. I wasn't judging…just guiding. I asked him to describe what he felt like at every financial juncture. I wanted him to relive those moments so he could recognize the emotion the next time and control it. After twenty minutes, Trey began to recognize that every one of his impulse purchases were tied to feelings of low self-esteem or, in his own words, "his arrogance."

The Business Dictionary defines impulse buying as "a spur of the moment, unplanned decision to buy made just before a purchase." Research findings suggest that emotions and feelings play a decisive role in purchasing, triggered by seeing the product or upon exposure to a well-crafted promotional message. Such purchases range from small – chocolate, clothing, magazines – to substantially large – jewelry, vehicles, works of art. About 80% of the time, these impulse buys lead to problems such as financial difficulties, family disapproval or feelings of guilt or disappointment.

For example, Trey described a vacation in Miami where they stayed at the Ritz-Carlton (they got a deal on a $1,000 a night room for $750 a night!). While strolling through a local mall, they were drawn to a Gucci store display window. Having recently received a bonus, Trey felt like they could splurge and "treat" themselves because they worked hard and deserved nice things (Money Reparations script).

The justification for the impulse buy was the usual, *"I deserve this because…"* Let me help you avoid becoming like Trey. Do not act on impulse when you hear yourself start a sentence with, *"I deserve this because…"* in a retail establishment.

In recalling the story, Trey said he felt bad immediately

upon leaving the Gucci store, but he did not tell his wife. Instead, he decided to even the playing field and convinced her they should see what her favorite designer Louis Vuitton had to offer. The truth is, she really didn't want anything special that day, but Trey pushed her, saying that she deserved a treat, too (his emotion) and they could swing it because he just received his bonus. She complied and picked up a new, very expensive bag. These items were purchased based on a negative emotion in Trey. He bought his wife a bag out of guilt for spending too much money on himself. If he was smarter, when he experienced the guilt, he should have returned the Gucci apparel and left the mall that much wealthier.

The good news is that Trey experienced a breakthrough by examining his money-motions and scripts. I referred him to a job opportunity that allowed him to get back on his feet. I made sure he had the financial resources he needed to ride the storm and even helped him negotiate his debt to manageable levels. Today, the couple is making six figures again, but they have a more frugal mentality, resulting in more money in their investment streams. Trey plans to buy income-producing real estate once his credit heals from the foreclosure. God worked it out in the end when Trey's spirit was ripened for improved stewardship.

We Need Community Support to Overcome Community-Wide Addiction

So many Black people make money decisions based on the Money Reparations script, claiming, "I *deserve this.*" Perhaps the historic and systemic lock out of many opportunities has led us to develop a mentality where buying stuff ministers to our souls. It makes us feel happy.

Scientifically, happiness releases dopamine. But who among us really understands how dopamine works? Many people think that dopamine is released when the brain receives a reward, but dopamine is actually released in *anticipation* of a reward. It's the dopamine that keeps the lab animal continuing to press a bar in its cage to be rewarded until the treat arrives.[2]

Therefore, we get a dopamine buzz as soon as our brain anticipates a treat. It happens when we look at the display window. The minute we enter the mall and start thinking we are going to buy something, dopamine works against us. We get an emotional high. This is especially problematic for people who started life in a hole and truly need to feel good about themselves. Shopping temporarily eases the pain until the bill comes due or the debt accumulates and then they feel even worse. I told you this is a sickness. This is the kind of dangerous cycle Trey and his wife entered into. This is the negative emotion cycle that led me to bankruptcy and perhaps it's what has you reading this book.

Inventory must be taken, money-motions examined and money scripts recognized in addition to discipline. Second, it requires emotional support. The Bible offers much wisdom and direction on practicing greater stewardship.[3]

The secret sauce of the Peloton brand is support. My friend and business coach, Ann Zaprazny, says that Pelotons' popularity is a master class in culture and how people crave

> Excessive spending is an addiction, but overcoming it is not impossible. First it requires self-examination.

community and support. The Peloton bike is overpriced. But people don't buy the bike they buy into the coaches and classes. They buy the community. Likewise, Ally Love, a Peloton instructor and entrepreneur, launched the tag line "Endurance is your superpower." Consider that quote for a moment...endurance is your superpower: mental, physical, relational, spiritual and financial endurance.

To have endurance in any area of your life, YOU have to commit to self-care and you need a community to support you. This is why *The Culture of Money* is about community alignment. We all need each other to do this. Black people will not survive the Great Financial Tsunami heading our way, now much faster after COVID-19, if we don't support positive financial behaviors more than we do having status.

A Windfall of Cash Won't Change Your Behaviors

If you can master your money-motions, you will be able to master money. Did you hear that? Mastering money is first about understanding why you do what you do, and your money- motions. This is the first step. Then it's recognizing and monitoring the money scripts that are auto playing when you are in the marketplace.

Notice I did not say that the first step to financial healing is receiving a windfall of cash or an inheritance. Why? It's simple. There is a long list of horror stories about lottery winners who die broke; pro athletes who made millions and end up bankrupt; celebrities who lived great lavish lifestyles in the limelight but lost it all. We all probably know at least one professional who always had a great job, made great money, but always cried broke. Why is this? Money can't change behaviors; money will only illuminate them. Whatever a person does with a little money is what they do with a lot of it.

You believed the lie, if in your head, it sounded like this, "If I had more money, I'd..."

> The greatest lie the devil ever told you was, "If you had more money, you'd be different."

There was a person who attended my church for years. She made easily $80,000 a year but was never generous. She always said that her budget was too tight to bless the church or help other parishioners. She said that one day if the good Lord above would bless her, then she would be in a better position to be a Blessor. Well, the good Lord did bless her. She inherited a lot of money.

Two weeks later, she asked for a meeting to tell me she was leaving the church because she did not believe in the need to give to a church. The truth is, this person was never going to be generous with a windfall because she had an unexamined financial illness. She needed money therapy. There were reasons she acted the way she did, but they were not being investigated and dealt with. The point is, all the money in the world will not change you. You must get your money-motions in check and identify your money scripts in order to change. If you do so, you will move into better position to reach your financial goals.

FOUR

Own Your Money Truth

Hopefully by reading this, something's been triggered in you. There's a part of you screaming out saying, "No! I don't want to go down in a burning inferno of debt and poverty!" I pray your spirit is already shifting and rejecting the future potential heart attacks, ulcers, high blood pressure and all the other psychosomatic symptoms that come from worrying about your money. I pray you are ready to be delivered from the money-motions of greed, fear, shame, embarrassment, false hope and wishing. I pray you are ready to better manage your money scripts so that they don't destroy your financial future.

Don't forget your dreams and the lifestyle you desire to live. They will come to pass only if you own your truth. Owning your truth empowers your faith and results in works. James, Jesus' brother, writes that *"Faith without action is not good"* (James 2:14). One Bible translation says that such behavior is *"not profitable."* I think this translation really brings alive this principle of faith in respect to financial healing.

A dear friend and spiritual mentor asked me to visit his sick mother in the hospital. Her name was "Mother Betty." As you know, in the Black church every woman over 60 is automatically respectfully called mother something, whether she's your momma or not. It is our way of honoring their wisdom. Mother Betty, like so many faithful Black people, entered the church doors every Sunday. She shouted, she prayed and she praised her way through so many trials. God did deliver, as she would say, "On time and every time." Mother Betty found herself in the hospital after a bad heart attack (not that there is a good one). She found out she was in need of triple bypass surgery.

I loved her sense of humor, great stories and incredible faith, so it was not a bother for me to visit her as often as I could. On my first visit, before I could say hello, she said, "Hey man of *gawd*, don't worry about me. My faith is strong and God will bring me out of this mess just like He did the last time!" I smiled and said, "Mother, I have no doubt God will do what He does, but what will you do? Will your faith have the works to back up a healing and walk in it?" She looked confused by my question. I asked her about the state of her diet and exercise before the attack. Like many in our community, sick and dying before their time, she looked at me as if I was speaking of Kryptonite and she was Superwoman!

She admitted that this wasn't her first heart attack and that the doctor told her to change her diet and walk daily. She confessed that she almost died before, but God healed her by faith. After a few more testimonies, I said, "Mother, I mean no disrespect, but if you believe God healed you, why did you not honor him by walking in your healing and practicing better stewardship of your body?" Now, before you call me disrespectful, I must tell you that one of her testimonies was about how much she loves soul food and just can't give it up, even though her diet was killing her. She also asked if I could sneak her some world-famous Brothers BBQ (Whitney Houston's favorite Newark, NJ, spot back in the day) because the hospital food was nasty.

She paused and said, "God knows I'm weak in that area, but he did it before and he will do it again." Mother's surgery went well. She was released. But she died a year later from another heart attack. Her diet never changed. Mother had faith, but no works. God certainly honored her prayers, but she failed to honor him with her actions.

Do you think your faith alone will bring you out of the financial mess you are in and heal you? Then your immaturity is showing: you are not ready for abundance yet. Even if you were blessed with a windfall of cash, you'd blow it unless you knew how to be a good steward. In respect to money, faith is no good without actions. You must be ready to shift and start to back up your prayers with faithful actions. In other words, if you pray for rain, start leaving your house with an umbrella every day until rain happens. Praying for rain and believing it will happen is part of your faith. Preparing for the rain by grabbing an umbrella is the action that releases favor on your life.

Many people confuse faith with the type of false hoping and wishing I discussed earlier: they think they believe, but they really don't. Remember, to get what you've never had you must do what you've never done. Reading this book might enlighten you, but taking action on what you read will shift your life straight into *the culture of money.*

Faith Demands You Do the Work on Yourself

You will not change until you are ready for action. Yes, change begins on the inside. It's a shift in emotions, outlook and thoughts, but it must manifest into external actions as well—*knowing more, owning more and passing down more.* You can read all the personal finance books and articles on the library shelf. You can learn all the tried-and-true principles, such as save 10% to 20% of your income to build an emergency savings fund. But knowing these principles does not matter until you are actually ready to be healed; to change your lifestyle. Don't be like Mother, asking God to get you out of your financial mess and yet stay as you are.

Some people treat personal finance just like they treat physical health; like the people who order every diet machine or workout gadget and never use it. When they see a new thing, the idea immediately comes to their heads, "Oh, the ab flex. I want it. Oh, the bend over backwards pull up thing. I want it." And you know what these machines are going to do already. They are going to gather dust in people's closets, and those people are going to remain overweight. They will eventually get sick from poor diet and lack of exercise to find themselves, yet again, standing in the need for prayer. Why? Because, like dear old Mother, they don't want to change. They have faith, but no works.

Likewise, anyone who reads this book will do the same thing with their money until they get tired of being sick and tired. *Something's gotta give!* I'll say it and shout it from the mountaintop until your faith is ready for action. *God does not want you living under great financial weight and stress!* God did not make you to live with financial weight and stress either.

Financial healing is available for you right now, but you must be ready to walk in it. You must be ready to shift and adopt the three simple values to *know more, own more and pass down more.* You must be ready to not just think and speak differently but *be different!* It's time to disrupt your life and create a new financial path.

Disruption 1: Do More Than Pray on It!

Humans are naturally prone to move from pain toward pleasure. Most people want to avoid pain at all costs. Unfortunately, when it comes to money, avoiding short-term pain will cause far greater long-term financial damage. Whatever bill, debt or unrealized financial goal is weighing heavily on you at this very moment is probably, in part, tied to your human nature to avoid pain in the past and seek pleasure.

People gamble and play lotteries to avoid a present

financial pain. Yet by doing so, they are only exacerbating the problem. Do you see the catch-22? Avoiding pain today delays your better positioning in the future. Your prayer alone won't solve your financial illness. Even God expects you to put action behind your faith to achieve a more profitable life.

By now you know that this book will help you make your life more rewarding and allow you to have experiences that others only dream about. You will be able to treat yourself to the finer things in life, shop at designer stores without hurting your financial future, vacation nicely, be generous…but first, you must grow your financial knowledge, invest in appreciable assets to own and execute a plan to pass your wealth down.

None of this is possible unless you shift; unless you heal. *Knowing more, owning more* and *passing down more* will put you in the best position to reach healthy goals.

Are you asking yourself, "What will it take?" It takes learning to delay pleasure and embrace a little emotional pain. If you walk in a deliverance from the money-motions of fear, greed, shame, embarrassment, false hoping and wishing, you will prosper. It's what's happening on the inside with your money scripts that is killing your future. You've allowed these negative emotions and scripts to ruin your mental, physical and spiritual health. You are missing out on the good life to live a fake one because you don't want to deal with the pain of examining yourself, challenging your emotions and changing behaviors.

Nobody likes to change. In his book called *Leadership*

Pain: The Classroom for Growth, Dr. Samuel R. Chand eloquently expands upon Don Cousins' groundbreaking *Leadershift* by breaking down the formula and the psychological reason why people don't like to change negative behaviors. Dr. Chand's proposition is very simple: Everybody wants to grow and increase, but people don't change because change hurts. Growth requires change, but change requires pain. Our human tendency is to avoid pain, so by default, we are avoiding growth and breakthroughs.

It is routine for people to remain in a bad situation because the pain of change keeps them there. I once had a terrible pain in my mouth. Turns out, I needed two root canals and extended oral surgery. After hearing the surgeon describe the process and recovery, I opted to delay it. I went to work daily in oral pain. As long as the pain in my mouth seemed less than the future pain I imagined in my recovery, I made no changes. It was not until the pain in my mouth became unbearable that I finally opted to change my dental situation.

I'm not alone.

We all know at least one couple in an unhappy relationship that should not be dating. Each individual complains about the other's behavior and continually decrees that they are leaving their lover. They don't belong together but neither of them can bear the pain of being alone, so they stay in a bad situation for years. Some of these relationships are abusive and all of them emotionally damaging. Yet, couples stay together because the prospect of a future with unknown pain is too great to bear.

Likewise, at least one guy reading this book has hidden the truth about his financial situation. As the family breadwinner, he can't bear the pain of telling his wife and kids they can no longer afford the life they have been living so they are still out shopping and racking up bills.

He is too afraid to deal with the future, so he begs, borrows and uses credit to live a lie. He may eventually lose the house and his family because he doesn't want to have the tough conversations and institute the changes necessary to survive. Change hurts and our mind tries to avoid pain at all costs. It is this parlor game you are playing with your money-motions that is slowly destroying you from the inside out.

For the longest time, I knew I needed to lose weight. My doctor had been warning me of my borderline diabetes for years. I knew I wanted to live without diabetes. I knew that with a better diet and more exercise I could avoid being on medication. Yet for some reason, I did nothing but what I had been doing all along – eating lots of junk food and high-starch food, especially late at night. I continued to work intensely all day chasing success. My success was my justification for why I could not workout regularly. I also knew that since I had so much sugar in my body, cutting starches and sugars out of my diet would cause me great withdrawal pains. I knew this because, when I attempted a 40-day, faith-based, Daniel fast (fruits, nuts, vegetables and water), I spent the first week in great pain without ingesting sugar (you all know sugar is edible crack, right?). The hardest part for me was starting the diet because I knew my body would feel bad and that the cravings and desires would plague me.

People with financial illness stay stuck for similar reasons. The hardest part of starting a new wealth-building lifestyle is the fear of pain. You want the growth, the increase and the wealth; you just don't want the pain that comes along with it. What pain? The great sacrifice of impressing others as well as yourself. How will you cope when you begin to live more frugally? You work so hard, don't you deserve the best stuff? Yes, but not today.

Today, you are sick. You need healing. You need to change. Like post-operative recovery, it will hurt for a little while, but in time you will feel better. The pain will subside, and you will be healed. Once you are healed you will live a better life. You deserve your best life, so embrace the pain. Change and overcome the emotions controlling our financial behaviors and make the shift toward being in control.

Disruption 2: Embrace a New Identity

There can be no behavioral change without behavioral identification. Lack is not solely about resources; it is also about the lack of examining your financial knowledge, your discipline to plan and the effort you put forth to work the plan. Lack is about living in old thinking that doesn't work versus renewing your mind.[1]

Being healed means living with a new identity. Sickness creates its own identity, and if you've been sick a long time, you may not know how to live healed. After Emancipation, some slaves stayed working on the plantations of their slave masters simply because that was the only life they knew. There was a certain comfort in familiarity, even if it was a painful familiarity. Likewise, financial illness creates an identity that must be torn down and replaced with a built-up new one. The old public persona must be rejected and a new one embraced.

The culture of money is all about embracing your new identity; someone who values financial knowledge, manages money in a way that achieves financial freedom through ownership and is consumed with legacy. This is your new identity – to *know more, own more and pass down more.*

Identity is powerful. It is about knowing who you are and your purpose. I started this book with a simple proverb that says a "righteous man" passes down wealth. Your healed identity is walking in that righteousness and good stewardship, where you live your whole life from this day forward with margin. Leave some leftovers in the fridge and pass wealth down. This focus has to become more than a goal, wish or dream, but a reality to live by daily. Consume yourself with the simple thought that, "everything in my life must bring harvest."

Identity is about your values and beliefs. What are the things most important to you? What inspires you at your core? The old you was inspired by feeling good, impressing others, greed and self-medicating emotional wounds with spending. The new you values knowledge, wealth creation and wealth transfer.

Identity is about embracing personal growth. Value the pain that comes with change. Focus on living your best life in reality; not posting on Instagram or tweeting hashtags. Start working hard, saving a lot, investing more and setting up your family and loved ones for a better life than you lived previously. Like me, you are inspired at your core by seeing Black people do well.

- You desire to see our people uplifted
- You desire to see us be the head and not the tail; the lender, not the borrower
- You desire to see us with the economic influence to control our own destiny
- You desire to see us have more seats at the table. You will do your part to make sure your kids don't miss out on the greatest wealth transfer in human history, whether it's today or in the future

Identity is about your capabilities. Understand the skills you have now and which skills you will need to live your new identity. It's about a new capacity for progress. The old you made excuses and found comfort in financial ignorance. The new you must refuse to be in the dark about anything, especially financial matters. The old you felt overwhelmed by finances and financial matters. The new you must relish the opportunity for empowerment and believes all things can be done.

Identity is about behavior. The old you never examined

emotions and connected them to financial behaviors (*money-motions*) so you suffered. The new you must embrace the daily actions that can help lead you to self-control, delayed spending, savings goals, investing and reading everything you can get your hands on about money.

Identity is about environment. The old you never truly broke down how your environment impacted you financially other than complaining about its contribution to your present situation. The new you is less concerned with where you started from, but more consumed with where you are going. You live by a plan that achieves a long-term financial goal. The new you must discover the environmental changes that will help you achieve your goals. To do this, perhaps invest in a smaller home in a less-affluent neighborhood. The new you will do whatever it takes to get to the goal. The new you should desire to be around money-smart people, while the old you was satisfied with living better than the previous generation or others in your family. The new you is concerned about living as an inspiration. You need to shift environments to follow your financial lead.

Living healed is living new. Leave the broke identity behind as you turn this page and live *the culture of money.* Solomon wrote, *"So a man thinks, so is he."* This means you are what you think of yourself. If you think you can't get ahead, you won't. Faith, wisdom and works must all come together in your newly formed financial identity where you commit to *know more, own more and pass down more.*

Disruption 3: See Change as Process

It's time to evaluate how ready you are to change your financial behaviors and adopt *the culture of money*. Many financial educators like me use the transtheoretical model developed by Prochaska and DiClemente. I base my business coaching and financial education classes on this model, which provides a framework to assess participants' readiness to change their financial behavior for the positive. To encourage you to adopt *the culture of money*, I want you to assess yourself. The goal is to acknowledge where you see yourself in the progression of change and move toward the final stages. There are various behaviors almost everyone goes through when experiencing change.

Stage One: Precontemplation. A person in the precontemplation stage does not intend to take action in the near future. This person will read this book, nod his head, think to himself, "hmmm" and won't do a thing with the new information. It's like when a reverend preaches the paint off the walls every Sunday (at least by the opinion of some); he or she knows that some people listening will do nothing with the Word.

I remember preaching a series called "Power Marriage." It provided a step-by-step plan to improve marital communication. My basic premise was that all couples will fight – there is no way to avoid it but they need to learn how to fight to win a better relationship versus win the argument. I presented a simple model to diffuse tension, deal with real issues and lay the groundwork for healing. We had a sermon guide with fill-in the blanks to help retention. I felt that most of the audience was taking it all in.

Two days after the series ended, a woman from the audience contacted my assistant to schedule marriage counseling for her and her spouse. When my assistant asked in what area of marriage, they were seeking counseling, she said, "We are struggling to communicate with each other." When my assistant shared the message with me, I looked at my wife and exclaimed, "You can't make this stuff up." She was there just two days before with her husband and hadn't retained *anything*. The sermon was streaming for replay on the web the next day, yet she still claimed they needed help.

Let's keep it real: they had sat through the entire sermon and had not paid attention to the Word that could have changed their home life. They were also a bit lazy since they didn't go online to watch the replay and take notes. I guess their serial TV habits watching *Basketball Wives* or *First Take* episodes got in their way.

Often the same thing happens whenever people encounter important new knowledge. Many in this stage are unaware that their behavior is problematic. Often, they are in denial or even delusional. They are struggling financially, need financial healing and yet they do nothing to better their situation! Their response? "Who cares," "It won't help," or "It's a waste of time." You are in stage one if you are having similar thoughts while reading this book. If you are, admit it. I can agree with you on one thing. *The culture of money* will do nothing for you if you stay in stage one.

The only way to move from this stage is to become more self-aware. Ask yourself, "Where am I? Am I onboard with adopting *the culture of money* for my household or will I stay in financial hell?"

The other thing that will move you along from stage one is to consider the long-term implications of staying where you are. The fact is, nothing will change if you stay put; pressing forward with a sense of urgency is the shift. Yes, in the past I filed bankruptcy. For many years, I lived with so much shame, but it did help me realize that my life was not meant to be bankrupt. I needed to change, both spiritually and fiscally. I needed to stop talking about it and start being about it.

I have a friend Reggie from the island of Antigua. About 15 years ago, he told me he was going to become a millionaire and showed me a picture of the mansion he was going to live in. Cool. I was onboard. I love visualizing what we are dreaming. I love setting goals, especially financial ones. I told Reggie how awesome his vision was and that I'd pray for him to achieve it and help him anyway I could.

A couple years later, I ran into Reggie again and I asked how his millionaire dream was going. Reggie told me he was still going to be a millionaire and this time he told me God gave him a vision and confirmed it. Again I said, "Cool, let's get after it."

Several more years passed before I ran into Reggie again and asked about his vision from heaven. Reggie said the same stuff he had said four years earlier, but he still had done nothing. The sad news is now, fifteen years later, Reggie is not a millionaire and has yet to move into that beautiful mansion he showed me. Even worse, Reggie is in financial ruin, having spent most of his money unsuitably. He is in the same apartment claiming the same promise. Do you get the picture? He's stuck in stage one because he refuses to see the long-term impact of talking the talk but not walking the walk.

Everyone is in one of these stages, but most are in stage one and won't do anything about their financial mess other than pray, cry, complain and sulk over the situation. They will always be seeking a blessing and yet live beneath their privilege.

Stage Two: Contemplation. This is when you begin to realize your behavior is problematic. The clearest sign of stage two is when you begin to look at the benefits and drawbacks of your continued financial behaviors. If my writing has done a good enough job, by now you may have already started this kind of self-reflection: taking inventory of where you are, how you got there and considering your future financial ruin by staying on the same course.

Stage Three: Preparation. This is a transition stage when you intend to take action. This is the true deliverance stage when you embrace the pain of personal growth and lifestyle change. You begin to feel like Popeye: "You've taken all you can stand until you can't *stand* no more!" Commitments to take action, to do *something*, you finally got the message: staying the same is financial hell and it's not safe to live like this anymore!

Changing financial behaviors requires buy-in to the need

to do something about your present situation. It is a new will to live better with a new wealth identity and less financial stress. Another sign you are in this stage is a fresh new appetite for financial knowledge with less clicking on Bossip, TMZ and ESPN and more on Financial Samurai, NerdWallet, The Motley Fool and Black Enterprise to learn more about money. The best you can do if you are in stage three is to recognize that you simply lack direction. A great financial education will instill confidence in your money skills as you work toward your wealth goals.

Stage Four: Action. You are in this stage if you have already made some positive changes in lifestyle. You have more than faith. You also have works and can see the profit from that powerful combination.

- You've traded in the Benz to get a decent, used non-luxury vehicle with lower overall operating costs
- You've moved out of the giant house or apartment into one that allows you to still live nicely and create more savings
- You've stopped going to the club and buying expensive drinks and started going to church and drinking that free coffee in the lobby, probably saving at least $100 a month
- You've stopped buying designer things like Louis Vuitton simply because you recognize you've had enough of it and are in control of your money emotions. Financial logic and not financial emotion prevail

Stage Five: Maintenance. You are in this stage when behaviors are changed, and life is lived with a plan to remain disciplined to your new identity. Just like healthy eating, it's one thing to lose the weight, but it's another to maintain the weight lost.

As I mentioned earlier, a few years ago I went on a Keto diet and lost about 25 pounds in two months. The only problem is I gained back 15 pounds within four weeks of reaching my diet goals. Why? I had no plan to maintain my weight loss. I was happy with the diet results versus pursuing a lifestyle shift. I started the Keto plan again to knock off those pounds, but this time I did more research and came up with a way to transition to a healthy maintenance eating plan. This time the weight stayed off.

Losing physical weight is a great comparison to losing debt and bills. Paying off a big credit card bill does not make it all over. If you don't hold on to deliverance, you might cheat the process and go back to buying on credit and find yourself right back in financial hell, sick again. That's why people in this stage begin to budget seriously and track expenses regularly. This is the most important stage to get to stewardship. The discipline of this stage is to avoid getting arrogant and avoid financial relapse into past negative behaviors.

Stage Six: Termination. This final stage is when you become healed fully. Your positive financial behavior changes are in place. You have moved beyond any temptation to go back to your old identity, succumb to negative money emotions and terrible financial behavior patterns. You have grown beyond the temptation to live broke like the old identity. You buy only what you can afford until you get to the desired level where you can entertain such treats with no regrets. You refuse to live for the Instagram post lie or coworkers' envy. You are determined to live in the exceedingly abundant life until the day you die.

This is the stage where people like you live *the culture of money* lifestyle. You value *knowing more, owning more* and *passing down more.* Your mentality has shifted toward investment and return in everything. You've become consumed with worth and not income. Your greatest desire is to be generous to others and pass wealth down to beautiful Black children.

Of course, the risk of financial relapse is always present. Remember "being broke" is like being an addict. Even when you get clean, there is always a chance you could relapse if you don't stick with the plan. Please don't be a poverty addict!

It's only when you reach this stage of financial behavior that you can consider yourself a financial success story. The termination phase is like having the ability to be around smokers but not smoke again. This is real financial healing.

Being a financial success is not about the amount of money you have, it's about *the culture of money* you subscribe to. It's about being able to leave a positive financial legacy, making the right financial decisions daily and ignoring the internal pressures to "look good" in front of people.

When it comes to planning for your financial future, in which stage of change stage are you?

Disruption 4: Develop Better Sight to Make Better Moves

Earlier, I presented the connection between money and emotions and challenged you to reflect. Now, to move forward with the challenge, you must allow yourself to dream an incredible financial dream. You probably have one already that sounds like, "I want to be rich," "I want to retire young," or "I want no financial stress." Nothing is wrong with those dreams, but you need to go deeper and begin to visualize the details of what gets you to your dream. *"A person is what they think"* (Proverbs 23:7).

As you pray for and receive a new financial dream, consider the intended versus the actual outcomes. Don't just visualize everything going according to plan. See what happens if you don't stick to the downloaded plan.

> If you only think about the big picture without visualizing the journey, you will struggle to live the dream.

For example, it's great to dream that you want to own your business and have freedom. It's even more powerful to think of yourself doing it all alone – but with no coach or outside help, you run the risk of making management mistakes and running your business into the ground. Consider what it would be like if you could find someone to help remove your blind spots, guide your entry to business management, avoid common pitfalls and access more capital. How much faster and easier would it be to achieve the dream?

Here's another scenario: Your dream is to be wealthy and

sip sweet tea on the beach in Nevis with no financial worries in the world. Now – visualize what it will take to get you there. Figure out how much you will need to save out of every paycheck. I'll bet you have started visualizing yourself:

- Setting up the automatic deposit from your paycheck into an investment account
- Working overtime and partying much less so you can squeeze every dime into savings
- Saying "no" to bailing out everybody so you can finally get ahead. Research proves this is one of the top reasons why middle-class Black people are behind their White middle-class counterparts
- See yourself doing this for 20 years! Then contrast that with seeing yourself doing the opposite and ruining the dream

It is important that you have foresight and tap into your emotions *before* you start the journey. By experiencing the stress, worry, anxiety and depression resulting from decisions that lead to a poor outcome, you condition yourself to desire the more excellent scenario. You get a better picture of what it will take. Visualizing your journey will help you learn, so that you might apply more wisdom in financial decisions.

What are your goals, dreams and motivators? Unlocking these thoughts will give you the passion and discipline you need to live a happier life. Developing better sight is what helped me get out of bankruptcy. I was so depressed after being told by the judge I was worth nothing in a public courtroom full of strangers. My bankruptcy was a blessing in disguise because it caused me to reflect on my emotions and money. It caused me to want to understand how, at 21 years old, I could be in this situation. I finally achieved a degree, had a good corporate paying job and was able to get out of the ghetto, yet I screwed it all up. Reflection led me to a season of intense prayer. In my opinion, prayer is a major part of reflection because God knows more about us than we can admit to ourselves.

In my prayer and reflection season, my greed, selfishness, narcissism and insecurities became fully exposed. What was also exposed was my spiritual immaturity. That is when I realized I had known God my whole life, but I didn't really know God. I lived my life as I wished and only invited him in when I was in trouble or needed something. This time was different. Embarrassed and humbled, I was broken. It was a perfect time for Him to speak to me.

Real prayer includes more listening than it does speaking or thinking. I repented and then my sight from heaven started. It was only then that God spoke to me and gave me a vision of a better and more beautiful financial future. He showed me that I'd never starve or beg for anything if I matured to live my best life.

I received a vision. Like the many blind men in the Bible, I could now see. I shared it with my wife Terri. I began to dream in prayer and see the details of my obedience or disobedience to the financial laws of stewardship of my faith, family and finances. It was during this season that I considered how I'd feel if I repeated the behaviors of my past. With all my senses I relived the embarrassing feeling of bankruptcy. Envisioning both the positive and negative results made me sure that I didn't want to go through that again. The result is that I'm living the dream.

Redemption is possible in all areas of our lives. I'm a strong believer that how we handle our money can be a strong indicator of our spiritual maturity.

My dream is nearly twenty years old, and it was created before vision boards became a "thing." The Proverbs teach a man is what he thinks. Habakkuk the prophet is the creator of the vision board. He teaches us to write down, visualize and display the vision so that we can run further "with it."

That is exactly what I did with my vision board, which can be as simple as a piece of poster board or a cork board onto which you affix imagery and words that relate to your future goals. If one of your goals is to buy a house in three years, you might include images of your dream home. If you want to retire and travel the world, include pictures of your intended destinations.

I plotted out how many years Terri and I intended to work, how we would fund our children's college education and when we planned to retire. I encourage you to create your own vision board, which will help inspire you to plan ahead. The real benefit of a vision board is having a little fun while planning your future. Plus, you'll be focusing on visual outcomes rather than getting bogged down in the process.

Here are some ideas to help you get started:

- Spend some time thinking and dreaming about your goals
- Find images, quotes or words that inspire you - check out magazines, online photos or you can draw the images yourself
- Think about emotion, not just objects. For example, how will you feel when you reach your dream of purchasing your own home?

Disruption 5: Set Higher Expectations for Yourself

Tyler Perry is a perfect example of the American dream and pursuing what God shows you. Despite living through a difficult, abusive childhood, Perry built the empire that he dreamed about, attracted massive audiences and built communities. He's also known for inspirational quotes, including two of my favorites. The first quote says: *"My biggest success is getting over the things that have tried to destroy and take me out of this life. Those are my biggest successes. It has nothing to do with work."* This quote perfectly challenges the emotions driving you away from financial success – reflection and change. The second quote is also apropos: *"Every dreamer in this room, there are people whose lives are tied to your dream. Own your stuff, own your business, own your way."* This speaks to owning your more prosperous future.

Raise the bar for what you think you can do. I am

challenging you to reach a new level of financial shrewdness by changing the way you think and behave. Why water down the topic? We are intelligent people who have achieved great things and setting a money culture individually, for our family or community, is the next logical step.

I pray you expect early retirement. To pass down hundreds of thousands of dollars. To pay off your home and live debt free. To finally see your student loans gone. If you expect only a little, you will get only a little out of your life.

Do you dream of what you could do if you had more? What do you need to do to get more? What if you were the one who invested in the next stock market bull run and rode it all the way into fortune? What if you brought real estate cheap and held it until appreciation?

You need to identify strong reasons to become financially healed. I do this regularly. This activity helps me relate money to the ability to live my desired lifestyle. This type of thinking provides strong, personalized reasons for people to move toward Stage 4: Action. You must own this. It's time to disrupt your life and adopt a wealth mentality. Stop talking about Black excellence and be excellent in your financial affairs.

If everyone reading this book moves to action, as a people we will have a better wealth identity. Now that the foundation is laid, I want to unpack the three community-wide values from *the culture of money*: that as a people we *know more, own more and pass down more*.

FIVE

What You Don't Know Is
Killing You

Regardless of what a few Black and Hispanic puppets say, President Donald Trump is a clear warning sign that we need to get our financial houses in order. It's clear that his view of people of color is that our existence has less value than other people. Pre-Covid19 he touted that Black unemployment was at historic lows. What he wasn't saying was that it remained higher than White unemployment! We can assume whatever gains he claimed for Blacks have been decimated by the Coronavirus.

What he's not saying is that it remains higher than White people! Is he really doing better in office? No. He has not balanced the scales at all. In fact, he's made things worse for us. He doesn't mention that Black people still face systemic discrimination, have less wealth, lower incomes, own less real estate and attract much less venture equity than Whites. What he's not saying is that Black home ownership (the #1 way to transfer wealth) has hit an all-time low,[1] and that his policies, especially COVID-19 related, will widen an already catastrophic wealth gap. His policies hurt the disadvantaged and the few Black and Hispanic people that escape his wrath must have means. In other words, there is always an allowance for "some" to make it as long as the masses are under control. This is the classic White supremacist allowance.

Playtime is over. We are facing down the greatest wealth transfer in history and my spirit is vexed that many of us still don't get it. We as a community are mainly consumers, not owners. We are not taking enough risks to venture out into wealth building, nor are we making the sacrifices necessary to play the wealth game right. This is because many of us don't know enough about money to be as frightened to death as we should. If you really understood what was happening in this country, you would prepare yourself for the financial hurricane of the ages. It will last for generations, not just a mere season. If you and your family get left behind after reading this book, then it's your fault. You must own that.

Do you know what else you must own? Your current level of financial knowledge. While racism is a legit systemic obstacle, racists can no longer stop Black people from consuming financial information and building financial knowledge. My message is simple – gain more financial knowledge, *own more* appreciable assets and pass more wealth down. Anyone can play this wealth game, but it must be played right.

If you are like most Americans, I bet you think you *know more* about money than you actually do and that's probably a big reason why you keep repeating the same negative financial behaviors. According to a survey, almost three-quarters (71%) of U.S. adults gave themselves a high rating regarding how much they knew about general finance topics. The funny thing is that most of them failed a six-question quiz about basic financial topics like diversification, compound interest and inflation.

Do you think you can get 100%? Test your knowledge at www.usfinancialcapability.org.

While you think you have financial knowledge, there's a good chance you don't know as much as you think you do, and the reality is your financial confidence is low. You might be one of the 40% who answered at least four questions correctly, but you are probably not in the 7% who answered all six questions correctly.[2]

That's why I had to introduce you to money psychology, so you can now understand the reasons behind what you have done in the past, and you can make the shift into new behaviors. Now you must put on your big girl or boy pants and own your situation. And so, then your financial health begins.

Personality drives behavior and behavior is what you do. Behaviors are influenced by what you know and what you know is influenced by what you've been exposed to. That's why we start with a core value to *know more*.

While within this book *knowing more* applies to financial knowledge, don't restrict yourself. Adopting a core value to pursue knowledge will bless you in every area of life. Herein, *know more* is simple speak for fundamentally agreeing as a community to be financial knowledge seekers; to be hungry and to satisfy your hunger with the food of new breakthrough information. It means to be able to answer six basic financial questions and get most of them correct with confidence and knowing. Faith without works is dead. If you want to live the blessed life, then put in the work and become a student of money. Can you stand to be blessed?

A mature person should seek after and value knowledge without neglecting the truth. You should seek to grab it, hold on to it and know that great knowledge can keep you from ruin. This is the trumpet Hosea is blowing.

The Bible is also a great source of financial knowledge. With over 2,000 scriptures about money, it would seem that God desires to bless us with more financial knowledge than most of us are willing to value and consume. More than any other people, we should be benefiting from all the Bible, including its ability to lead us to financial healing. God knew we would need financial knowledge, so he made the Bible chock full of it.

Financial knowledge thwarts financial ignorance. It removes blind spots, so we can do better. It does not guarantee we will do better, that depends on your level of initiative, but it opens the potential to better decision making.

New financial knowledge creates better potential outcomes if it's made actionable. Black people, like the Nation of Israel, have experienced an Exodus, so we should especially be reminded of this call to free ourselves from the bondage of financial ignorance.

It's ironic that our ancestors did not have access to as much information as we do now, but what they did know was a simple truth: *know more*. They believed in educating themselves to get ahead. It was the will of God to remove ignorance from their lives. They taught this lesson to their children. People sacrificed hard days in the fields for the hope that their hard work would allow a young mind to get better exposed, more educated, more knowledge, make more money and leave the fields behind. Their logic was Bible based because it was all they knew.

What You Don't Know Is Killing You – Truth!

Hosea warns that the result of not valuing knowledge is destruction. You will end up in financial ruin because you lack financial knowledge. Any reasonably intelligent person can see that ignorance isn't bliss; it destroys opportunities, potential and futures. Not knowing is a problem. Not knowing about money is hurting us more disproportionately.

I applaud the new generation of Black athletes and celebrities who are leading the financial knowledge revolution. People like Will Smith, basketball's Andre Iguodala and Rihanna are refusing to just stay in their creative or athletic lanes: they are becoming very knowledgeable about managing and building their wealth. They've seen so many Black entertainers and athletes before them leave the public eye broke by trusting others to have knowledge for them. This philosophy brought many to ruin. Sammy Davis, Redd Foxx,

Fantasia and most recently rapper T-Pain spoke of being in the limelight but being broke because of what they did not know. Adrian Peterson, a future Hall of Fame NFL running back, made over $100 million playing football, but due to financial mismanagement and trusting the wrong people, at one time, he was broke. I don't even need to know the details. There's only one way this could happen. His fortune was destroyed for his lack of financial knowledge. Low financial knowledge equals low financial confidence, which forces you to rely upon the knowledge of others. That's great if those you rely upon can be trusted but it is financial ruin if they have ulterior motives.

Never trust people to make money decisions for you when you are completely ignorant and can't comprehend what they are doing. In other words, you must always know enough to understand that *something* isn't right with your money. You don't have to be the smartest person in the world to know that you should not invest your money in anything you can't understand – like bitcoin, forex, precious metals or commodities. No matter what the promised returns, they are run from complicated schemes that are above your head.

Financial predators will prey upon the money-motions of greed, false hopes and wishes to get you to make a decision that will hurt you. They know that *what you don't know will hurt you* and that's exactly what they aim to do. Too many pyramid and Ponzi schemes have taken advantage of so many in our community. Churches, clubs and community groups have all fallen victim to the wolf in sheep's clothing promising fortunes with a scheme no one truly understands. The financially ignorant have no shot at a bright financial future unless they get lucky or blessed, which depends on their worldview.

The culture of money is about always seeking to remove the boundaries of financial ignorance that cause destruction in our lives and embrace the pursuit of financial knowledge. It's not for those who want to be left behind in the greatest wealth transfer in history.

While financial illiteracy is not an issue unique to any one population, it affects the Black community even more, men and women, young and old, across all socioeconomic lines. We can't ignore it any longer, our economic future and resulting power in the U.S. depends on it.

We May Suffer from Lack of Financial Confidence

I have a friend named Rey who is about 45 years old, married and has a couple of children. Ray lives in the suburbs, makes a decent living and at one time was easily making big money working for a global entertainment company. About 10 years ago, Rey lost the big bucks and the big job and had to reinvent himself in another field. I asked Ray a simple question regarding his personal finances: "Do you know what to do with your money, but just don't do it?" He asked me to share his response with you because it is very enlightening and gets at the core reason we need *the culture of money,* so please don't think I'm putting his business in the streets!

Rey said, "A lot of people just don't admit they need financial help. I think the reason we don't admit the need for help is because we're embarrassed and have very little confidence in this area. Even with me, there are things that I learned later that were bad financial decisions and I kicked myself for not knowing it before the financial error. I'm like, 'Why didn't I know this?' I think a lot of people hide behind the excuse that 'they didn't know'."

Rey's sentiments are not only his own. I think they represent a lot of us at one stage or another in our financial journey. A few years after college, I was asking myself the same question, "Why didn't I know?" Why didn't I know that you don't buy a new car that depreciates as soon as you drive it off the lot when you can buy a quality, pre-owned one with a warranty for much less? Why didn't I know that you don't buy the biggest house in the neighborhood, thus causing the values of everyone else's smaller homes to increase while you probably won't get what you paid for it on resale because there are so few high range comparables?

Why didn't I know that putting as much money in your 401(k) plan with a company match as soon as you started working was more important than investing in the stock market directly? Why didn't I understand how valuable free invested money was to my future by taking advantage of my company's 401(k) match? Why did I think I was being so smart opening my little investment account and picking bad stocks when there was a company giving me money every time I invested money (tax-free, no less)? Why did I have so little financial confidence as an adult?

Why? Why? Why? The list could go on and on with all the things I didn't know about money until hundreds of bad decisions later. What about you? How long is the list of things you didn't know about money until after you messed up? Maybe you are blessed and have never regretted the financial decisions you've made, but so many people can't claim that testimony. There are many people who live with regret tied to a long list of bad money decisions; many, if not all, tied to their lack of knowledge and resulting lack of financial confidence.

Like Rey, we all suffer from lack of confidence, one way or another. If we really examine our financial choices, many of us might feel like we could have done better if we knew better.

The real question you should wrestle with is "Why do you not know more"? Why do you have so little financial confidence? Furthermore, why were you so comfortable not knowing in the first place? Why haven't you've been driven to consume knowledge before consuming "stuff"? It all begins with this: ignorance isn't bliss, knowledge is blessed.

Financial Knowledge Removes Financial Fears

Generally speaking, the more knowledge a person has, the more confidence they have on a subject. Likewise, the less a person understands, the more he will develop fear based on insecurity. One of my sons was working with a math tutor to increase his grades in school. He has always been a great student, but math was more struggle than ease. During a regular session the tutor gave him a short word problem to complete. My son worked through the problem at a good pace and completed it. Right before handing it over for grading, he changed his answer. The tutor smirked and said, "You have the wrong answer," as soon as my son gave him the paper. My son responded, "How do you know, you didn't even grade it yet." The tutor replied, "I was watching you the whole time and your work was great, you actually had the right answer, but you second-guess yourself because your confidence is low. You have low math confidence because of your past math challenges in class. You need to trust your instinct more."

This is exactly what happens when you have had past financial challenges. You second guess yourself constantly because your money insecurity is high. Many develop high levels of money insecurity because they blew it in the past. They blew it in the past because they didn't have the financial knowledge or positive money behaviors to operate in high confidence. They don't trust their instinct.

Someone who doesn't understand money develops financial fear. This leads them to freeze up or act too fast when it comes to financial decision-making. This is called a negative money cycle. A financially ignorant person then doubles down on this negative cycle with a belief that they won't make the same mistake twice.

Small business guru Michael E. Gerber, author of *The E-*

Myth: Why Most Businesses Don't Work and What to Do About It, once asked me a question in a telephone conversation many years ago. I had built my insurance brokerage to a level of repute within the industry and that's when Michael asked me, "Do you know what can ruin your business and take you out quickly?" I hesitated to respond because I knew I was talking to the small business guru, so I wanted to be sure. After many guesses, he finally stopped me and said, "I don't know your business and what can take you out, but neither do you, which means you are not good at what you do, you are just lucky! When you are good, you know what can take you out and you do all you can to avoid that. When you are lucky, you just ride the wave and hope it never goes away. Usually these people run their businesses into the ground because they do not put the work in to know what can ruin their dream. They are idiots. Don't be an idiot. Start to study your business."

True wisdom from a small business guru applies to more than entrepreneurship; it also applies to life. What you don't know will kill you. Knowing more is everything. This issue surfaces when luck runs out and the truth is revealed that you made a terrible financial decision, which now sets back all of your plans. You probably experienced this feeling after buying something you couldn't truly afford while living on a Walmart budget. When exposure happens, along come those negative money emotions—regret, shame, fear, embarrassment and worry—which can lead you to freeze up when making future financial decisions. This fear freeze is a negative cycle that is symptomatic of not knowing more. It leads to making the same mistakes over and over again. This behavior is typical of a person who knows he shouldn't buy "it" but still does.

Who Do You Secretly Blame for Your Financial Disasters?

Avoiding issues makes you weak, but owning your stuff makes you stronger. Honestly, perhaps you don't know more about money because you don't *want* to know. The average person is afraid to discuss money, especially with others. Some people don't discuss money openly because they don't want to come off as arrogant or braggadocious. Others don't discuss money openly because they don't want to be shamed, so they fake it until they make it. Yet, others struggle to place enough value on financial knowledge because they are blinded by blame.

Blame is a dangerous game, since it removes the focus from *your* contribution to the contributions of others. Who do we all secretly blame for poor financial knowledge? Truth be told, our parents and schools, in that order.

Blame is how we roll. In our minds, most problems we face today are often our parents' fault. The reason a man is a philanderer is often tied to his daddy being a rolling stone. The reason a woman is sometimes considered not good enough is because her parents made her feel that way. That is not to say the aforementioned causes aren't major contributors – of course they are! But they may not be the sole contributors to your present issue. When it comes to money, you may often feel like Rey: "Why didn't anybody tell me the information I needed to know?"

After you make your list of names, then answer this question: Who do you blame for your present lack of ownership for poor financial knowledge? Now that you are grown, can it still be your parents' fault that you are not taking financial education seriously? Is it still their fault that you have a decent job and no retirement strategy?

There are so many players we can find to be at fault in our demise, including the old Lord of the Flies Beelzebub himself! We can't forget to blame the retailers and advertisers for bombarding and tempting us with stuff to buy. While we are at it, let's put some blame on the credit card companies for making it far too easy to get credit as a freshman in college. Don't forget to blame the pastor – he or she is supposed to preach you into salvation and help you get rich too, right? There are so many people to blame. Perhaps some may have contributed to your lack of financial knowledge, but so have you. That needs to change.

Here's what I mean. Of course, your parents are the first people who taught you about money. But is it fair to blame them for not telling you what you needed to know?

I'm almost fifty years old and both my parents are over seventy, which means they were born before 1945. My parents did not have access to the plethora of financial information I have now. They had no blogs, few magazines and no television networks or radio stations dedicated to wealth building within the Black community. Most of what they learned was passed-down folk wisdom on what the preacher taught over the pulpit.

Most of my parents' generation had meager means and were only a few generations removed from slavery. My parents can blame *their* parents, who also had limited access to financial education in the early 20th century. The blame game can reach all the way back to us leaving the plantation.

What if your ancestors grew up during The Great Depression? That was a terrible season for all Americans, but especially Black people. Most of us were locked out of investing in the stock market. But because we were undereducated and discriminated against, we were not likely to get the job competing with unemployed Whites who had bottomed out. Racism combined with systematic oppression ravaged Black communities. What money education could these Black survivors have passed down?

- *"Don't invest in the stock market; you can lose everything you have in a day."*

- *"Don't put your money in banks; they can't be trusted."*

- *"Don't start a business, it's too risky; the money can all be lost in one economic downturn, so just get a good job and stay put."*

Here's my point: my great, great granddad could have only passed down and exposed his family to wealth wisdom and proper behaviors if he had access to and practiced them. It's hard to keep blaming our ancestors for what they did not know. Someone must take responsibility for what is happening presently, which is the focus for the culture money movement. You have the power and capability to *know more*, so why don't you?

Own the fact that you have access to more information and education than your ancestors ever had, and you can be more financially capable than they could have ever been, so move on.

The second blame is aimed at the school system and frankly, if there is any entity to be blamed, it should be this one. Schools don't teach financial education. Most don't even teach home economics anymore, which was a staple when I was younger.

Schools have found a way to teach everything under the sun except the one thing that is the most practical and needed – financial education. More affluent communities can get away with this because the parents there were probably exposed to privilege, so they know how to teach little Chatsworth, Skylar or Hunter about finances. Unfortunately, the lack of financial education has a far more disparate impact in less-advantaged communities.

These communities need more financial education, especially since there are fewer positive role models for wealth building and the children may be less likely to learn it through home practices. Even if they do have parents with great money habits and strong financial education, those parents may never earn enough money to make ends meet on the most disciplined budgets. So, the kids will not get to see wealth-building behaviors modeled to the fullest extent.

We can agree that the education system has failed us in the area of financial education, however, are parents and schools to blame for individuals who know they are financially ill, continue to walk around with the sickness and refuse any treatment? Are they to blame for people who are so comfortable as financially ignorant that they don't want to know more? These people have access to all the information in the world but decide not to consume it, no matter how it will help them. No sir. People who live without tuning in to financial education are more to blame than any one thing.

> A man must examine himself and change for the better. *Knowing more* is where it starts.

Financial Illiteracy Costs Us Billions

I want to prove to you that there is a financial cost to not *knowing more*. After the Great Recession of 2008, you would think we would have learned our lesson in regard to using money more wisely and securing our source(s) of income. But I'm not so sure we have. According to the Federal Reserve in 2019, Americans owe a record $1.04 trillion in credit card debt–up from less than $854 billion five years ago. Doesn't look like we've learned from our mistakes, does it?

That's a lot of money that needs to be repaid in the future! It's a lot of money on credit. It is money we spent that we didn't have. It's money that we still owe with post-pandemic economy and another recession bearing down on us.

You can only imagine the number of studies and reports that have been done analyzing the effects of the most recent Great Recession. Psychologists, sociologists, financial experts, investors, real estate developers and many other subject-matter experts have dissected the event to see how it has affected and changed the way we think and live—or if it actually had an impact. Here is just a very small sampling of what these studies have shown:

Your job and your skills are your greatest assets. No matter how strong or weak the economy is, if you have a paycheck coming in, you have some measure of security. You can provide the basics for yourself and your family. You can never have too many skills. High skill level and great work ethic are recession shields. I have never let go of a highly skilled hard worker in a recession – I simply can't afford to. Remember this: dead weight goes first.

Downsizing is an option. You might have to go from 3,000-square-feet to 1,000-square-feet of living space, but you'll still have housing. You may eat PB&J sandwiches every day and buy store-brand canned veggies instead of organic everything, but you'll still have food to eat. You may shop at discount stores or second-hand boutiques, but as long as your purchases are neat, clean and in good repair, you can still look great *sans* the designer labels.

Just because you can, doesn't mean you should – borrow money, that is. Over-borrowing was one of the main causes of the recession. People borrowed as much as they qualified for but didn't repay it. They couldn't. Because even though their income *said* they were good for it (and had the means to pay it back), they didn't. The monies were either already allocated for other things or they paid the minimum amount necessary; giving them even more to spend (so they thought).

Poor financial education is at the root of most bad loans, especially predatory lending like payday loans, rent-to-buy agreements and high-interest car loans and mortgages that take advantage of Black communities. Here are a couple of real-life examples of how not knowing more can bring on financial ruin.

Steve and Karen were told they qualified for a mortgage loan that would stretch their budget to the max with not one bit of "wiggle room." But they were told that if they took out a balloon mortgage, they could afford it with no problems. A balloon mortgage is where you get a lower payment upfront, usually only paying the monthly interest due on the loan balance until a later point in time, when a large payment is due.

These loans are popular with people who want more house than their paycheck can really handle. The balloon portion refers to the large, lump-sum payment usually due in three to ten years. Most people who *think* they are fiscally smart, figure that they will have plenty of time to refinance the home before the balloon payment is due. The problem with this logic is that before the balloon is due, they are only paying interest on the loan, so the principal balance never goes down. Unless values increase, they are not building equity. Their theory also assumes that they will be equally or more creditworthy when they are ready to refinance, which assumes they will be equally or better employed, making equal or greater dollars. Do you see where this is going?

The real estate agent and lender explained to Steve and Karen that a balloon mortgage would require them to pay only the interest on the loan for three years, but at the end of those three years they would owe one, large lump-sum payment for the principal. The amount borrowed is the principal of a loan. Interest is calculated on the principal. The loan amortization schedule separates the principal and interest, so you can see which part of your monthly payment goes to paying off the principal versus interest. You should always request an amortization schedule from your lender prior to signing any loan documents.

Steve and Karen decided they would go for it because their car would be paid off in a year giving them that extra monthly cash to go toward the principal balloon payment they would have to make (both smart assumptions). They also agreed to put half the principal payment in savings each month toward their lump sum principal payment (really smart).

These ideas were great in *theory*, but here are a few things they didn't know: The car was in bad shape and wasn't worth much. They had to get rid of it and borrow money for another one. Their plan to use car payment money for principal money didn't pan out (it usually never does for the financially ill).

The real estate agent convinced them they would most likely get raises each year. She told them if they would put that money away and pretend it wasn't there, they would likely end up with around $2,000 saved. In practice, Karen received only one raise in three years. Steve was fired from two different jobs and ended up working for just over minimum wage. It's just not a good idea to plan on money that you don't have. I'm not saying the real estate agent was the devil, but she sounded just like him by saying, "Get what you want; it will just work out for you."

When the three years were up, they had less than $5,000 of the $50,000 they needed. In the end, they lost the house. On paper it appeared they could barely afford it. Based on what they made and what they were already spending each month, there was no way they could have saved enough for that balloon lump sum payment – not even if they could have existed on beans and cornbread or bologna sandwiches. They lost the house they should never have been allowed to "purchase" because they were not as smart as they thought they were. They had no counsel of wise men or women. They did no research. They needed to kn*ow more,* but they didn't and it cost them.

Then there's **Anthony and Nina,** who are another example of what can happen when you borrow more than you should because of your lack of financial knowledge. Anthony was in the Army and had just returned from a tour in Afghanistan. He and Nina were newlyweds just learning how to manage their money.

The car salesman "saw them coming." He convinced this sweet, trusting pair to buy a car that was $4,000 more than what they had decided they could afford before they drove onto the lot (smart). The salesman convinced them that if they stretched the payments out over six years they'd be in great shape. And like so many do, they fell for the financial sales pitch (not a smart move).

The payments were still more than they were comfortable with, but they were doable. However, the problem was that they could have paid for the car they originally wanted in three years and had all that money to put in savings or toward something else. The car is now not worth what they still owe on it – even though they will finally pay it off this year.

Anthony and Nina learned the hard (and very expensive) way that just because you can borrow money doesn't mean you should. They learned that *knowing more* has the direct benefit of saving real dollars, getting better terms, increasing wealth and living better.

There are more financial horror stories than these pages could hold regarding people being duped because they simply don't value financial knowledge. Consider these stats that further speak to this phenomenon:

Adult Statistics

- 81% of Americans said they don't know how much money they'll need to fund their golden years (Bank of America; Merrill Lynch). Black people aren't even thinking about their golden years; we just hope that when we die, someone can raise money for our funerals

- 40% of respondents said they either could not cover an emergency expense of $400, (according to a new report by the Federal Reserve, May 2019). The Fed found that 27% of survey respondents would have to borrow money or sell something to cover a $400 emergency – 12% couldn't cover it at all. Many Black people have no savings – The "last hired, first fired" syndrome combined with our poor financial habits add up to the perfect storm to leave us unable to respond to emergencies

- 31% of adults report they have no savings (Harris Poll). We spend too much disposable income on depreciating, worthless assets

Youth Statistics

- Almost 50% of millennials don't believe they could come up with $2,000 within the next month if an emergency arose (PricewaterhouseCoopers [PwC])

- Nearly two-thirds of Americans (62%) are stressed about money (American Psychological Association) Only 16% of Americans between ages 18-26 are very optimistic about their financial futures (Bank of America)

Higher Education Statistics

- 11.5% of 2014 college graduates have loans in default (U.S. Department of Education)

- 81% of college-educated millennials have at least one long-standing debt (PwC)

- The average debt of students when they graduated from college rose from $18,550 to $28,950 (last reported), an increase of 56% (TICAS)

Lottery Games: The Stock Market for the Financially Uneducated

This part of our discussion will be painful but necessary. I grew up in an environment where people played "the numbers," but even as a kid I knew it was wasteful. There would usually be a dude in the hood that simply came around with a little notebook and wrote down "numbers" you picked to hit on the street lottery (obviously run by gangsters). Even as a kid, I wondered why people played a game where the person writing the numbers gets to control which number "hits."

Today, there are bodegas and corner stores in Harlem and in the Bronx that sell so many scratch-offs they have tables and chairs in the back of the store. The store owners know the lottery mentality is the manifestation of a financial illness, yet they are more than willing to cooperate with a person's demise, as long as they get their commission from the state.

Remember the money scripts we discussed earlier? The Money Vigilance script would never allow you to play the lottery as a means to build serious wealth. It's a game of chance which can only be poorly underwritten. Gambling and investing may mean the same thing to people who don't *know more*. Someone with *the culture of money* mindset would not risk potential investment capital on something with such low odds of return and a high risk of loss.

Why is the lottery attractive to the financially ill and uneducated? False hoping and wishing. A good deal of people understandably dream of hitting big, but the chances are not in their favor. You might not care much about losing a few dollars, but the losses start to add up and they could become serious if you have a gambling problem. Plus, even if you do win, there is so much more you could have done with the money you spent on lottery for all those years.

A Powerball drawing in Tennessee once had a one-in-292-million chance of winning. That means you had a better chance of being hit by lighting (one in 2.3 million) or being bitten by a snake or dying from an airplane engine falling on your head from the sky on your way to work (one in 10 million) than winning the Powerball.

Yes, someone has to win, eventually, and you can't win it unless you are in it (that's how they hook you). Chances of winning the lottery are remote, but that doesn't stop 57% of adults from spending $80 billion a year playing.[3]

The lottery is not just one of those fun things we do to strike it rich. It simply drains income and is financially foolish, especially for Blacks. According to recent statistics, the majority of players are part of the lower economic classes. The lottery is part of an oppressive system that takes advantage of the financially uneducated and why many financial gurus call it a "poverty tax."

Here's the real problem: we are over-represented in the lottery market and severely under-represented in the stock market. Studies show that low Black participation in the stock market contributes to the widening wealth gap between Black and White households.[4] Just look at the statistical breakdown among those groups owning taxable investment accounts: 22% of Blacks, 25% of Hispanics, 36% of Whites and 47% of Asians.[5]

The good news is that some of us are starting to up our investing game. According to a 2017 Ariel Investment market research report, about 67% of Blacks with incomes of at least $50,000 have money invested in stocks or stock mutual funds.

> Although there are no guarantees in the stock market, the likelihood of getting a return on your investment is far better than your chances of winning the lottery.

That compares with 60% in 2010 and 57% in 1998. These

figures are noteworthy for celebration but while our participation percentage has increased, our total invested dollars is still underwhelming.

Listen while I repeat: the lottery is not how you get rich, it's how you waste money. Investing is the way wealth has been built for ages. To prove my point, consider the following scenario comparing investing in the market versus wasting money in the lottery.

Spending $5 per week on lottery tickets adds up to $260 per year. Over twenty years (a typical long-term investment horizon for stocks and bonds), the total spent on lottery tickets would add up to $5,200 spent. Meanwhile, investing $260 per year in stocks earning 7.3% annually (based on equities' historical performance) yields $11,015 earnings after twenty years. Due to risk, your earnings in the stock market may go up and down, but if you just spent money on lottery tickets and presumably won nothing, you would be $5,200 out-of-pocket after twenty years.[6]

I've heard many people complain that their money situation is too tight to be able to save and invest, yet they exhibit the "discipline" to play the lottery or visit casinos regularly. Why do so many people comfortably exhibit and repeat such a negative money behavior? As I have said before – they are ignorant but don't know it and are okay with it.

I know Black people who regularly spend $20+ dollars a week playing lotteries, yet they don't even have a personal investment account. You can't do that and ever expect to be rich. Most rich folks don't play lotteries because they know those games are wasteful and the return on investment is little to none.

Investments work on an entirely different principle than gambling. Investments offer you the ability to research and underwrite a stock, business or property purchase. Meanwhile, the lottery and casino gaming are based on pure luck, offering you little to no ability to control the odds. Investments are ownership. A lottery ticket is owning a piece of paper that's not even worth the amount you gambled by the next day.

We need to shift our culture from being okay with gaming and lotteries. They hurt our communities. Every state promises gaming will bring jobs and revitalize urban areas, yet there is no place in Black America where we can say, "Job well done." Get serious! Accept that while both lotteries/gaming and investing entail risk, only one of them can guarantee a long-term capital gain if you are consistent, disciplined and start early.

Investing values "owning" over "gambling." Ads by the state gaming commissions make winning the lottery so attractive, but statistically, the odds of that kind of "investing" make no sense. Many fall to temptation, spending their money on hoping and wishing versus investing, or worse, not even meeting basic needs (food, clothing and housing) or education, which can provide opportunities for earning more income.

Building wealth is not just about raising the money that you earn; it is about understanding how to best use your dollars to make more dollars. Avoiding the lottery and gambling hazard is a good place to start.

Bad Credit Equals a Worse Job

Just because the words "credit card" and "cash" begin with the letter C doesn't mean they are the same thing. When you pay cash for something, it's done and over with. It's yours by rights. When you swipe or insert a credit card, the purchase is not yours…not yet, anyway. You still have to pay for it later with cold, hard cash. You are basically buying time, as well as, taking two steps for one purchase. Save the two-step for the dance floor and pay cash whenever possible.

This is another exercise in helping you learn the difference between needs and wants. When you hand over and let go of actual cash, you tend to think twice about whether you really need to purchase the item or service you were coveting before reaching into your wallet.

In a recent study, adults ages 35 to 54 were asked, "Have you ever been turned down for a job or promotion as a result of your credit or financial background"? At least 5% said they knew for sure that was the reason. Another 18% responded "not sure," but believed their current or past financial situations definitely contributed to not being hired.

Be honest. Did you have any idea prior to reading the previous paragraph that your finances could actually affect your hire-ability? And did you know your financial condition can also affect the price you pay for numerous essential goods and services?

Your credit score, which is the grade you earn based on how well you pay your bills and debts, plays a key role in what it costs you to borrow money and to obtain a sizeable number of goods and services. Many industries base your rates on the belief that the more responsible you are with your money, the more responsible you will be in general. Therefore, the higher your credit score, the lower your auto insurance, mortgage or loan interest rate may be. The same goes for...

- **Utility deposits.** When moving to a new home (especially in a new town), if your credit rate is high enough, you will often be excused from paying any deposit for hooking up the utilities in your home. This can literally save hundreds of dollars
- **Rent.** Some landlords will not rent to anyone with a credit rating less than 600 or 650. Those that do will usually require a higher deposit
- **Jobs.** It is worth mentioning again that you can be passed over for a job because of your credit score and other financial information

I know these things may seem a bit unfair and that there are often extenuating circumstances that can cause you to appear to be fiscally irresponsible when you really aren't. If this is the case, you need to be upfront when faced with any of the above situations. Otherwise, it may cost more than you ever imagined. Having proof of your "innocence" is also a good idea. But the very best idea of all is to take action now to do everything possible to keep a solid credit score. By now, you should know that what I mean by doing "everything possible" is getting your hustle budget on, even if, at least in the beginning, it is the "hustle of inconvenience."

Maybe your monthly pool of income seems more like your kids' wading pool—the one with the leak in it. That is why adding to your income is usually the most effective and efficient way to stop the leak.

Let's take a look at how you can use what income you have in the most effective manner, whether you hustle your budget or not, specifically by reviewing the logistics and best practices to use so you can pay down your debt. But before I get down to business, I want to remind you of the dangers of carrying unnecessary debt and not correctly handling the debt you have accumulated. Call it a scare tactic or shock effect. I call it doing whatever it takes to open your eyes and your mind to the truth.

Owing on credit cards is by far the most "popular" source of debt. It is right up there with mortgage and student loan debts. The facts and figures surrounding credit card debt may surprise you. The bulk of people carrying the debt are **not** from low-income families who aren't living within their means. Data gathered by a number of agencies, including CreditDonkey.com, reports just the opposite. A number of research reports and surveys share that the higher a person's income, the higher his credit card debt.

I agree this doesn't make a lot of sense. From where most of us are sitting, we believe we wouldn't have any problem living on what "they" make. But the numbers don't lie. When it comes to credit card debt:

- People with credit scores over 750 report paying the minimum balance on their card approximately two months out of the year
- The average American household is carrying over $6,000 in revolving credit card debt
- The total credit card debt in this country is over $830 billion
- Nearly 40% of people with credit cards pay the balance in full every month (This is the only smart way to use a credit card, so hats off to these people)
- The flipside: 29% of credit card users pay the minimum monthly payment or just slightly more. Doing so costs cardholders hundreds of dollars in interest each year
- Baby Boomers and Generation Xers carry the most credit card debt, averaging over $7,000 per household

Financial Education Is Easier Than H.S. Math

As a certified financial education instructor and a preacher, I get the chance to teach about money regularly. Interestingly, one of the biggest objections I've heard when teaching or counseling people, is that "financial stuff" is simply too hard to understand. I've heard this objection from the GED grad to the Ph.D.

Many people believe that you need to be exceptional at math to be good at money. Well, I'm not. I struggled with math all the way through college. I had to take statistics twice just to get a passing grade. But with calculators, YouTube videos, books and information everywhere, almost anything can be figured out. Remember, so a man thinks, so is he. The person who embraces limitation is limited.

Telling yourself, "I'm not good with numbers," is a very limiting belief and/or an excuse that will hurt your financial future. These days you don't need to do anything on paper; ask *Siri* or *Alexa* and they will do the math for you.

Knowing more is less about math than it is about developing wisdom, learning principles and practicing fiscal discipline. Math is not a requirement for having the confidence and financial capability to make the right moves every time!

You may argue that money topics are "just not your thing" or they are "too complicated and confusing." Eliminate these excuses from your vocabulary and remove the mental block inside your mind if you want to breakthrough. Increase your faith! Everything is hard for the person who never tries to push themselves to *know more*.

Truth is, money is easier than almost any high school subject and more interesting since it affects your lifestyle. The rote memorization required to complete a history class is way more intimidating than learning about money. Have you tried to help a middle school kid with math homework lately? You probably referred him to a tutor once you realized the subject matter was way above your head. Today, even college students face a world where what they learned in certain subjects is outdated by the time they graduate.

I hope you don't object to knowing more because you live by the YOLO philosophy (You Only Live Once). If so, you may fail to realize you can live once now and be broke in five years. YOLO is a short-sighted and financially damaging belief that will cause you to be comfortably ignorant. It's much better to commit to live well over and over again. That's why most YOLO people I know are broke.

Others create a mental block because of faith. They mean well but they have been incorrectly taught and subscribe to a theology that declares, *"Money is the root of all evil."* This is just wrong. It is based upon a misreading of 1 Timothy 6:6-10, *"The rebuke of false teachers who pursue earthly gain over teaching truth."*

Being financially astute, pursuing honest wealth gain, desiring a good retirement and living by a long-term financial plan are called great stewardship, which is completely faithful to scripture. These attributes are not the same as a "love" of money, which is akin to greed. You can pursue gain without "loving" money so much that it drives you to greed and causes you to neglect the truth.

Maybe in your mind you hear the same thing in a more secular way: *"Money can't buy happiness."* Having this view is just as limiting as the others mentioned since it is also a kind of misrepresentation. It is certainly not a good reason to remain financially illiterate.

No, money can't buy happiness, but in many ways, it can

buy peace! Let me make this clear. I've been broke with lots of problems. I am *rich* with problems. By the evidence of my life, I've anecdotally concluded that being rich with problems is much better than being broke with problems. Being broke magnifies and intensifies almost every problem. I'll take more money and more problems any day of the week!

Terri and I started our marriage in lack and now live in abundance. When I was poor even my little problems were big ones. Now many of the little problems are gone and I have peace. For example, when we first started out, if the washing machine broke, it was a major problem because we didn't have the savings to get a new one. We were also living paycheck to paycheck, so we didn't have the margin in our weekly take home pay to get the machine fixed for a long time. Now, if the machine broke today, I have peace in knowing that I can buy a new one or get it fixed ASAP; same problem, less worry. Moreover, I can now afford a service contract to make sure the machine stays operational. So no, money can't buy love or happiness, but it can bring some peace of mind that you need and deserve.

Desiring to *know more* about money can put you and yours in the best position to live your best life. No more lotteries and gambling to cover up the fact that you don't know enough about money to make a real financial plan. Start taking personal responsibility for your current lack of knowledge. Embrace *the culture of money*'s primary value to *know more*.

Remove Financial Insecurity. Usher in Money Mastery

Some will read the story I shared about small business guru Michael Gerber earlier and say, "Wow, what he said was harsh." Some of my brothers and sisters would be extra triggered because he was White and came off a certain way.

As you read it perhaps you even thought to yourself, "I wouldn't let anyone talk to me like that!" When I was on the phone with him, his directness took me back a little. Honestly, I did struggle with the race thing for a second. I thought, "Who does this White guy think he is talking down to me like that and telling me I was just lucky and not good!"

When I examine the thoughts I had at the time, it was my insecurities that were presenting themselves. Why would someone who had already made it even take the time to talk with me unless he really wanted to help? I didn't pay him for the call. I was introduced to him by my younger sister. Could you imagine if I allowed my personal insecurity to respond to Michael in an indignant or cold way? Moreover, what if I just tuned him out because I thought he was "Coming against me?" I would not have listened to one of the greatest counsels I had ever heard. He changed my life with that challenging sentence. He helped my business level up.

With one sentence he caused me to become a student of the entrepreneurship game. He spurred me to invest and open other businesses in a way that guaranteed thriving over just surviving. This all happened because I owned and rebuked my insecure thoughts, listened, learned and applied the knowledge he shared.

There is a simple formula for gaining exponential knowledge: a student must learn. To learn, a student must be taught. To be taught, a student must be challenged and criticized. To be challenged and criticized, a student must be bigger than his insecurities. I could've gotten upset with Gerber, but he was right. I learned, grew and prospered.

I hope that this book is challenging who you are as a person. I am challenging your existing *comfortable money* personality; attempting to tear it down by helping you build a brand new, more prosperous personality. Some of what you find in this book will not be actionable unless you remove insecurity and allow yourself to be challenged so you can usher in money mastery.

One of the reasons people don't challenge themselves to *know more* about money is their insecurity. Yes, many people are financially insecure. You can be financially secure but yet suffer from financial insecurity.

> Your lack of money is not your biggest issue. Your biggest issue is not having the confidence to know what to do with every single dollar that you come into contact with.

Financial insecurity comes from being unsure about your financial identity, goals and decision making. Insecure thoughts regarding money sound like, "Well, *I'm* not on that level" or "*I* don't make enough money to plan." Thoughts that sound like, "If I had money, I would..."

What is the point of hoping and praying for riches when you don't have the confidence to know what to do with the dollars you currently have?

Financial insecurity is a stronghold in our minds, passed down like a genetic disease from generation to generation. It rears its ugly head even when new information is presented. When I teach in some circles, I am customarily asked a litany of questions after speaking; in other circles, I hear nothing from the group but "that was a good word." I'm sure the same level of intelligent inquiry is happening in both circles, but one group is more secure using their public voices to gain clarity, especially when it comes to money.

Worrying about "putting your business in the streets" is harmful for those who want to usher in money mastery. Money masters have an insatiable appetite for *knowing more* and they are willing to ask the Michael Gerbers of the world a litany of questions in order to gain clarity and experience regular breakthroughs.

There Is No Dumb Financial Question

I'm challenging you to walk delivered from the kind of insecurity that causes you to live for others and avoid asking public questions.

When it comes to money, most of us don't ask; we pretend we know what we are talking about even when we don't. After speaking at a workshop, a woman approached me with a question about her company's 401(k). She asked me what a 401(k) was and whether she should invest in it. When I asked her, "Did the company bring the vendor in to explain the program?" She said, "Yes, we had a meeting where they explained everything to us, but most of it was over my head and I didn't want to seem dumb, so I didn't ask any questions."

I inquired further and asked, "Did other people ask questions?" Her response was, "Yes, they asked a lot of questions." I inquired again and asked, "Were you the only Black person in the room?" She replied, "No, there was one other in a room of about 200 employees."

Let's review this scenario. A professional, educated, smart Black woman had the opportunity to ask questions of a financial expert and she did not because she would feel "dumb," yet she felt comfortable asking me, a Black professional, privately. At least she did ask somebody eventually, so I'll give her credit. Now, in order to deal with the reasons why she might have those feelings in that room, we need to unpack a few truths about the White people in the room:

- They asked financial questions so theoretically left better armed to build wealth
- A majority of them felt "comfortable" with their public voice and were not concerned about being seen as "dumb"
- They asked advanced-level questions about "rollovers" and "self-directed" options, while my sistah didn't know what questions to ask!

It's well documented that White privilege leads to a

certain oblivious confidence and opportunity in respect to many things in American society. To be honest, I have also been in the faithful-few minority in a corporate presentation setting and I can confirm that I heard similar voices in my head. The voices told me that I would "seem stupid" in front of the White people in the room.

Here are a few questions we should consider while evaluating this all too familiar scenario:

- So, what if they think you are dumb? They can't stop you from learning, investing your paycheck or taking advantage of your 401(k) plan!
- What is more important? To *know more* so you leave armed with the info you need for a less stressful financial future or to live life on mute and enduring future poverty?
- How bad do you want to *know more, own more and pass down more?*
- Is your fear of investigating to find truth bigger than your desire for earning more than ever before?

Why do you care what "they" think, anyway? How does their response affect anything in your life?

My late father-in-law, Claude, used to exclaim, "There is no dumb question!" You need to challenge the low esteem that is holding back your financial future. You don't *know more* because you are not asking enough questions. You are muting your public voice at the wrong time. Your circle might include the same group of people who are also limited in financial knowledge and capability, so you all end up repeating the same terrible money behaviors. Please stop.

It's time to come out of your comfort zone and expand your circle. Don't be afraid to open up. Peeling off your insecurity will allow you to *know more* about money and everything else.

"They" don't matter. You do. God made you unique. You need to take authority over your financial future and start "asking" as many money questions as necessary to build your confidence.

The True Power of Financial Education

Promoting his recent book *Dapper Dan: Made in Harlem* on a talk show, Dapper Dan told a commanding story about the power of financial education and *knowing more*. Years ago, Dan's father took him to a department store to get his first suit and was going to buy it on credit. Dan's dad had less than a third-grade education but worked hard his whole life to give his family the best he could. Dan asked his father if he could read through the credit agreement. Even though he was only a kid, after reviewing the paperwork, he told his father not to buy him the suit because the agreement disclosed he would pay at least 2.5 times the cost of the suit by financing it. He and his father left the store. On their way out, Dan's father grabbed him and said with tears in his eyes, "You can read son." Dan knew that his father was proud that his son protected him from making a bad decision. With those few words, he was encouraging Dan to continue to use the power of education to make good financial decisions.

If you are not a student of money, then you may never have any. In the game of money, you must become a player on the field, not a fan in the stands. The player on the field is a student of the game. She watches films, reads playbooks and studies opponents' practices regularly. The same can be said for the money master. A money master is what I call a person who loves to *know more* and applies that knowledge. He is on the field, watching shows about money, reading financial books and articles and studying his money emotions. He sizes up the opponents by comparing their wealth gains and practices stewardship regularly. Some people talk about money and cheer from the stands loudly about how rich they are. As long as they remain cheerleading fans of money from the stands, they will never gain as much as those of us who put in the work on the field.

It's time for you to get out of the stands, stop *talking* about money and start *being* about it. Become a real player in this money game. Become a student of the game. All the greats in sports, business, ministry, social activism study how their heroes have made it in their respective fields. Who are *you* studying? What are you reading? If you were to assess yourself right now, have you just been a fan of money or are you playing the money game like a boss? Are you already a student of the money game?

Students of the money game are voracious readers. They

love making, saving, investing and spending money wisely. I have said it before and I'll say it again – everybody should read their Bible daily and after that, they should read financial literature. This is an area where we can all improve.

You can be destroyed by what you don't know. If you want to be a better money manager, you must do better reading financial literature to increase your confidence and comprehension. It's easier to learn about money, which we all love, than world history, which so many of us found boring in school. Money is easier to understand than high school calculus and biology. If you graduated high school, don't fool yourself, you can do this.

Notice I didn't title this section "becoming a financial reader." Why? Because reading and studying are not the same thing. Those who embrace *the culture of money* don't just read information, they study it, take notes and ask questions. They try to constantly experience breakthroughs and shift into action.

To study financial education means to either enroll in a financial education class (in class or online) or commit to reading and studying a financial magazine, blog or book every single week. Other than feeding your faith, is there any other topic you should be reading more about? If you fail to do this, you may potentially delay or destroy your financial plans, you may not be able to retire well and live the lifestyle you desire or pass money down to the next generation.

Money Masters Follow Money Coaches

You are not a student unless you study. Likewise, you are not a student unless you have a teacher or a coach. When it comes to money, I use the terms teacher, mentor and coach interchangeably. Teachers need not be alive nor within close proximity for you to become their student. There are people who watch my ministry online and then tell me how much they learned from the sermons. Technology allows us to learn from anywhere in the world today.

You have no excuse for missing out on money teachers or coaches. Whether you call them coach, adviser, teacher or role model, it doesn't matter. You need to follow someone who can regularly help you experience breakthroughs by removing your blind spots.

Players need coaches, fans don't. You are a fan if you are not being coached or taught. In this sense, mentoring and discipling are similar terms. Christian disciples are those who follow the true teachings of Jesus. One needs not to have physically shaken Jesus' hand to be discipled by his written Word. Likewise, you can commit yourself to following a money coach without having ever shaken hands.

Isn't it amazing that we have life coaches, business coaches, sports coaches and marriage coaches? Coaches are available for everything! What you really need is a money coach you will follow! Even churches coach new believers and make them disciples – yet discipleship programs often fall short of helping the faithful overcome the greatest stronghold and enemy of their lives – money! Churches can use *The*

Culture of Money: Wealth Track curriculum to disciple the faithful into financial health.

The whole point I'm making is that exposure is important. Exposure to new information triggers breakthroughs. Why? Because once you experience something new, you have a frame of reference, which means you can move from Stage One (Precontemplation) to Stage Four (Action) quickly.

Since Blacks historically trail other groups by a wide margin in inherited wealth and overall income, it's safe to conclude we've had fewer wealth role models until recently. Hallelujah! That narrative is changing for the better.

You may have chosen a money coach by osmosis if not by intention. Someone has taught you about money and there are behaviors you are modeling whether you know it or not. Think about what you have subconsciously learned from your money coaches up to this point in your life? Let's get a breakthrough by examining this question in three phases:

- Before age 18
- From ages 18 – 30
- From age 30 – now

While you think about this, I'll share a few stories of how exposure to money coaches, good and bad, has helped me experience breakthroughs or setbacks.

Before age 18. How much did I read about money? Absolutely *zero* financially-related magazines or books. I'd sum up my early years as Stage One – Precontemplation. I had very little knowledge in the brain bank. I knew that I didn't know a whole lot and I also didn't know what I didn't know. As for exposure to money coaches in Newark, NJ, most of the people I ran into with money were drug dealers and street hustlers. These were the coaches most of my peers wanted to emulate. I don't know if they had a lot or just showed off, but they had the best cars and the nicest clothes. What did they teach me? Make money and spend money! Show the world you've arrived. Drive the nicest car and look good, no matter what the cost.

I was also coached by my father who owned an auto body shop. His was positive money coaching. He taught me that anyone could make money if they knew how to hustle. My dad never finished grammar school, but he had his own business for over 30 years.

I was also subconsciously coached by the upper middle class and wealthy kids at my high school, Seton Hall Prep in West Orange, New Jersey. This is where I first started to learn about "the other side"; those that "had in excess." Most of the Black students who attended there came from hard-working blue-collar families like mine. We didn't have the option to just hang out at our summer house down the shore (a New Jersey phrase for going to the beach). In a weird way, the "had in excess" group helped me realize that having money could allow me to experience a whole new world. On the other hand, that group also helped me feel financially insecure in a major way. I felt like I was a third-class citizen who did not belong in their wealthy world. Perhaps this was the origin of my wanting to "show them."

I did not meet a single financial planner, millionaire, wealth expert or senior executive before age 18. I ended this period with very little money confidence, little knowledge and few positive money coaches. You are a product of the company you keep and in respect to money, I wasn't a well-formed product yet.

From ages 18-30. College reinforced my lack of financial knowledge. Trying to save for college was my first introduction to dealing with serious money matters. I felt insecure and ill-prepared for this since my high school did not teach us how to apply to college or financial aid. My guidance counselor tried to talk me into trade school, even though I was accepted into UCLA, Drew, Boston University and Rutgers! I didn't even know you could shop around for loans until *after* I graduated from college, so my plan from day one was to graduate in three years to cut the cost of tuition. I was the first student from Drew University to accomplish this feat while working 30 hours a week.

I started my first job at Chubb Insurance Company, making around $25,000 as an underwriter trainee. This is where I intentionally chose my first money coach, a tall Irish senior executive named Terry Cavanaugh. He taught me that the first thing I should do was to max out my 401(k) so I could get the very generous 5% company match. He told me if I just did that starting with my first check, I'd retire a millionaire, like him. This was my first exposure to wealth advice from someone with means.

Did I listen? Nope. I did not take his advice until almost seven years later, after I filed for bankruptcy. Rosemary, another coach who is still a lifelong friend, told me, "Don't spend it all in one place." Did I listen? Nope. I wanted to "fit in" again, so I spent a lot of my money on suits, shoes and watches. My first designer watch was a Raymond Weil for $3,000. Yes, now I know it was stupid to spend that kind of money. I spent over 10% of my annual, first-year gross salary on a watch to impress executives who didn't care about my future.

The executives used to discuss watches like it was a hobby, so I didn't want my Casio to come up in the conversation. I also upgraded my car and started buying my family extravagant gifts to validate my success. This behavior lasted for exactly 18 months after I graduated college.

Before I knew it, my mountain of credit card, student loan and car note debt, became an avalanche. I fell behind on payments for everything. Like most people in this situation, I was too ashamed to talk to anyone. My older sister Cynthia was furthering her path as a doctor and she had always been great with money. If you gave her $1 as a kid, she could stretch it because she was always thinking about needing it in her future. We were close and she had good habits. She could have been a money coach for me, but I was too embarrassed to ask for her advice before filing bankruptcy.

Of course, the bankruptcy attorney talked the talk and convinced me it was a no brainer to file because I was young and not really making real money yet so just get on with it. He was a bad money coach. I was bankrupt at 21. My highest monthly payment and debt was my student loans, which was eighty percent of the debt I was looking to get discharged. This was over 25 years ago, yet today, colleges are still piling debt onto unsuspecting students with little to no financial education.

My Personal Financial Knowledge Journey

My career path rendered me regular promotions and pay increases. The bankruptcy slowed me down a little, but there were more lessons to learn. The best thing it did was to get me to examine my behavior: why I did what I did. I had a divine vision about my future and began to understand God's more excellent way for my life. I adopted my older sister as a money coach. I began to model my behavior after her.

From age 30 to now. I was in Stage Four – Action. I became a daily consumer of personal finance articles, books and more. I started to turn the corner from surviving to thriving. Terri and I invested heavily in a 401(k). We bought two houses and had the means to give one to my parents. We started to invest excess capital in the stock market. We finally accumulated savings. By the time I was 26 I was making $165,000 a year. We had money in the bank, investments and home ownership. We could also regularly bless our extended family without setting us back.

This is when I made the big money move to join a Chubb competitor to start a new division as a Senior Vice President at Crum & Forster Insurance Company. The company paid me $200,000 plus a signing bonus to accept the job. The rest is history, right? No, later on I left them for a start-up opportunity in Manhattan to make $300,000 plus signing bonus.

This is the time I learned: you must be prepared for financial calamity. I was fired from the startup firm due to racial discrimination. We settled out of court and I used the settlement money to seed my first business, Professional Risk Solutions, in the fall of 2001. God has blessed me beyond my wildest dreams through this business move. I exceeded my five-year business plan in two years and it made me a millionaire (net worth) by 33!

This phase of increase in my life can be directly tied to the people who coached me, either directly or indirectly. This was the time where my setbacks pushed me from the stands as a fan of money to get on the field and play the game like a boss. This phase was also where I saw God blessing me with people and giving me people to bless.

Before, I thought my good fortune would just fall from the sky. I learned that God blesses us through people more than through things. Having better money coaches increased my knowledge and increased my wealth.

My entrepreneurial success gave me access to new people circles, wealth advice and investment opportunities. Most of my circles are people of influence and means. Here's the dirty little secret I will share: these individuals helped me remove my investing blind spots and shared intel on the best money moves to make. Through them, I've been introduced to private equity fund investing, and I became an accredited investor.

Notice the connection between opportunity and exposure. You get more opportunities in life with increased exposure to the right people. You get the opportunity to develop social capital. I know it doesn't seem fair, but it's true. From this exposure, I learned how to operate more than one business at a time and how to build multiple streams of income. I learned from other wealthy individuals the importance of paying the capital gain versus personal income tax rate. Capital gains tax rates are considerably lower than personal income tax rates. Capital gain taxes are assessed on the positive difference (gain) between the sale price of the asset and its original purchase price. For example, if you invest $100,000 to start a business and later sell it for $1,000,000, you pay a capital gains tax on the $900,000 gain. The capital gains tax assessment on the $900,000 gain ranges from 0% to 20%, depending on the state, for most assets held for more than a year. On the other hand, if you earned a $900,000 salary your personal income tax rate would range from 10% to 37%. Wouldn't you rather pay less taxes? Then think long-term asset appreciation over income.

Shift from An Income Mentality to A Wealth Mentality

Today, I'm more than okay with paying for financial knowledge. I have three accountants, four attorneys and a few coaches and planners to help me figure out how to protect my assets and pass them down the *correct* way. That is my sole focus. I am committed to not rely on the government to pay me reparations (although I do agree they owe me and *should* pay). I will not depend on public policy to solve my family's wealth gap. I've taken full ownership and by the grace of God, I have closed that gap for my kids.

I have shared the CliffsNotes® version of my personal financial journey only to prove to you that gaining exposure to money coaches will help change your life. Since you are subconsciously emulating potentially negative behaviors from unintentional money coaches, it's better for you to become more intentional about who you choose to speak to about your financial life. Be humble. You don't know it all and you don't need to as long as you know somebody who knows what you don't know.

The culture of money values knowing more. To *know more* you must read more and choose positive money coaches. My life changed because I was willing to examine myself, change my behaviors, acquire financial knowledge and expose myself to people who could help remove my blind spots. Only then could I experience breakthroughs regularly. I pray all of that happens for you, too.

Financial Education Is "Works" That Trigger Breakthroughs

Remember, faith without works is dead. It is not profitable. You must believe what you work and work what you believe. If you believe you are going to live a better financial life and leave a legacy, then commit to a better financial education. That is your first job.

When I was a kid, there was a commercial with the slogan, "Reading is Fundamental." This certainly applies to money mastery. Let's connect the money psychology from earlier to establish how reading and coaching lead to financial breakthroughs.

There are many iterations of what I am about to share with you, so understand that the concept of removing blind spots is not new. Most executive and leadership coaches teach something similar, although my theory is developed by combining business school teachings with biblical truth. There are two fundamental ways to learn new things and experience breakthroughs: spiritually, meaning by or from the Spirit[7] and naturally, meaning by or from another human.[8]

> Gaining financial wisdom is not for the sake of accumulating financial knowledge, but to learn how to use it.

Consider all the financial knowledge available in our universe and connect it to learning:

There are three levels of learning in our financial leadership that fit together to create knowledge, understanding and revelation. Level Three, Revelation, is where all financial breakthroughs take place.

- **Level One: Knowledge.** There is financial information you know. For example, you probably know that spending more than you earn is not a great idea.

You've heard it everywhere. Even if you don't put this knowledge to action, *you know that you know it.*

- **Level Two: Understanding.** *What we know we don't know* about money is the beginning of understanding. As you begin to grow in knowledge, new gaps are identified and you don't know how to grow beyond a certain point. You know you're missing something and you know it hinders you from leveling up. There is financial information you don't know. An example of this is something called APR. You may not know what it stands for or how it works. The fact is, this is a gap you can identify and work on by yourself because you've grown to be able to acquire and incorporate the knowledge out there. Understanding provides an even bigger breakthrough than knowledge.

- **Level Three: Revelation.** *What we don't know we don't know* about money. Revelation is the power behind preaching. It is the fire behind awakenings. These are unchartered waters where you need a guide to get you through. For example, many of you reading this book may not understand that accessing private equity investing is not easy for Blacks who do not have the social or economic capital to become accredited investors.

This was a revelation to me at one point in my financial education. To be an accredited investor, you must have a specific amount of income, assets and, depending on the level of investment, an accountant who can affirm your investment capability. Do you know what private equity is and why it is a super important part of higher returns for sophisticated investors? Did you know that an accountant can affirm your investment capability?

I hope you will take your Level One: Knowledge and investigate some of the terms I used above so that you can quickly get to Level Three to experience your own breakthrough. Experience Level Three: Revelation as much as possible. Sometimes the biggest obstacle to your financial success is not what you don't know. After all, you can always research what you don't know and get an understanding. Significant breakthroughs happen when your blind spots are removed through high-level learning, coaching or a spiritual revelation.

Learning and growth occur at all three levels, but the best financial breakthroughs occur when blind spots are removed. Knowing more is a commitment to removing financial blind spots! Everything you have read is to get you to shift into *the culture of money*.

Culture is based upon values and beliefs. To adopt this ideology, you need to make a few lifestyle shifts to live out the three core values. The first core value you must *know more* to have more. Simply put, this is placing a higher personal value of financial knowledge and learning. For the Black community, I place this value right after faith and family. We need to understand what is happening in the world and how money connects to everything. We need to understand that we can live the best life ever, but we must put actions behind our dreams.

What is the first thing you need to do? A simple goal is to commit a full hour a week to financial learning. Technology is changing everything, so this goal should be pretty easy to accomplish. By doing so, you will be able to increase your breakthroughs. By reading personal finance blogs and articles regularly you will be able to stay up to date on the latest apps that automate saving, investing and giving you more time to make more money doing your side hustles.

Don't just limit your studying to personal finance articles. Supplement those readings with anything you can get your hands on regarding developing a side hustle. I do not recommend that most of you quit your day job to become an entrepreneur. They are rarer than you think, and it is hard to start your own business. But, anyone and I mean anyone, can create multiple income streams via side hustles and investing. God has blessed each person with innumerable gifts, many of which can be monetized to create wealth. Unlocking this hidden potential begins with reading and learning.

For me, this includes reading scriptures on money as well. Money study should not *be* your faith life, but it should be *included* in your faith life. Why wouldn't you want to benefit from the wisdom the Bible offers and receive what the Spirit has to say? I see no separation in faith, family and finances: they are three concentric circles and each one affects the other. If you apply the Word, your life will change for the better today.

Your reading goal should include learning and understanding at least one new financial term a week. I highly recommend using Investopedia.com like a personal finance dictionary to discover everything you need to know about money.

Subscribe to a personal finance newsletter like the one I offer on my website. *The Culture of Money* newsletter offers a weekly digest of financial articles with my personal summary in language everyone can understand. I include the links to the original articles for further reading. The value of this is to get a capsule of information in layman's language to encourage you to learn more at your own pace. I also recommend the articles on websites like Financial Samurai, Nerd Wallet and The Motley Fool. There are countless others that may work better for you so check them all out.

Do something with your newfound knowledge. Connect everything to your personal goals and take action on information now that you are healed and free. This is what God wants. Faith without works is no profit. The next step is clear. You must have a financial plan to live your most blessed life.

The last time you attended school or sat in a classroom may have been ages ago. And the thought of picking up another workbook or sitting through a course may scare you to death. You may actually think that having your wisdom teeth extracted would be more pleasurable. But whether it is to further your education for professional reasons or to gain some valuable financial literacy, you need to push yourself toward this inconvenience. Take the time to do this. Do it for yourself and your family.

Do you wonder what I mean when I use the term "financial literacy" or how to get a financial education without pursuing a degree program on business and finance? Financial literacy leads to increasing your understanding of money and how it works. Becoming more financially literate can happen when you:

- Take a class on personal finance through your county extension office, a local college or vocational tech school, or through your church
- Learn how money works from a trusted banker, financial consultant or accountant
- Become a regular visitor to sites like Kiplinger.com and mymoney.gov
- Read articles and books on the subjects of adding a hustle to your budget, how to spend less than you make, debt reduction and financial planning for the future

These resources are your friends. You have to stop treating financial literacy resources like you treat working out or dieting. You know that no matter what the latest diet craze is, the diet itself isn't enough. You need to have some sort of daily workout routine in addition to eating a healthy diet and getting plenty of rest. With financial literacy you know you need to make an adequate income to meet your needs. You know you need to get out of debt, save for retirement and do some estate planning. But unless you have a proper balance of all these things, you may not achieve the desired outcome.

If you don't take financial literacy to the next level by using what you learn, it's worthless. Not only do you need to know how money works and how to make it work for you, but you need to understand the financial implications of all your decisions. It isn't enough to just know what you need to do. It is also not enough to cut a few corners or even make a little extra money on the side if you don't redistribute the money you save or use the added income wisely and purposefully.

I recently saw a website that offered the ability to test financial IQ. To date over 29,000 people have taken the test. An average score for 24- to 35-year-old person is a C.

Would you have been happy with a C grade in high school? Even if you were content with a C, would you be happy having an average knowledge of how to handle your finances? Are you willing to settle for an average existence and future? Wouldn't you like to have above-average financial knowledge, especially since I'm providing the information and access to resources to become a financial scholar?

Knowing more is committing to a lifetime of financial education. Trying to own a business, real estate and stock investments without a financial education is putting the cart before the horse. Trying to leave a legacy with limited to no financial education is false hoping and wishing. You will only leave debt and anger. I hope you embrace this value and allow it to influence your money-motions, money scripts and create a new habit of studying.

SIX

Own Or Be Owned

A Brief Black Wealth History

As a people, our Black ancestors used to be longer-term thinkers. They desired to own everything from land to businesses. They wanted control and worked hard as anybody to get it. Back then, the simple goal was to buy a piece of land and hold on to it. Racism prevented many of them from owning businesses outside the Black community, but many within the community persevered. Their neighborhoods were filled with more than Black-owned barbershops, salons and funeral homes. They included restaurants, clubs, mechanics, retailers, wholesalers, transportation and construction…you name it, they had it. "Buy Black" was the only option because in many locales they were not welcome to buy from White businesses.

Our ancestors understood the importance of saving for the singular purpose of ownership. Their #1 goal was to buy property. Even slaves would use their paltry free time in South Carolina to raise their own livestock. They grew crops to sell at market. The slaves who managed to get ahead often did so through collaboration and support. A group of six, ten or a dozen field hands might have used nights and weekends to plant cotton, which they sold when possible, and split the profits.

This very scenario occurred in 1853 in Rusk County, Texas. It wasn't uncommon for antebellum plantation owners to hire out their slaves for a year at a time. This system provided the opportunity for the most highly skilled and talented Blacks to be hired on their own time. They negotiated contracts, made their own living arrangements and paid their masters a specified amount, usually on a semi-annual or annual basis. A few enslaved men, such as Anthony Weston and Thomas Davis of South Carolina, established full-on enterprises. It should be emphasized, however, that this was not the norm. It was very difficult for any slave to engage in any kind of entrepreneurship. In the years leading up to the Civil War, free Blacks in the South took advantage of the economic downturn in the 1840s, and used it as a chance to buy land, build houses and open storefronts.

One of the major reasons certain Black communities grew so rapidly and prolifically from the late 19th to the mid-20th century was because institutionalized segregation necessitated the creation of a separate, closed-circuit economy. Dubois gives an example of this phenomenon in his 1912 essay "The Upbuilding of Black Durham":[1]

"Today there is a singular group in Durham where a black man may get up in the morning from a mattress made by black men, in a house which a Black man built out of lumber which Black men cut and planed; he may put on a suit which he bought at a colored haberdashery and socks knit at a colored mill; he may cook victuals from a colored grocery on a stove which Black men fashioned; he may earn his living working for colored men, be sick in a colored hospital and buried from a colored church; and the Negro insurance society will pay his widow enough to keep his children in a colored school. This is surely progress."

Ironically, racist laws provided opportunity for Black communities to flourish. There was a symbiotic relationship between Black businesses and Black religious, cultural and educational institutions. Black churches and businesses funded the establishment of historically Black colleges and universities (HBCUs), which provided a hub for Black scholars and professionals and a training ground for future entrepreneurs.[2]

However, in the age of Black codes and Jim Crow, this success did not come without risks. Neighborhoods were consistently and systematically dismantled by racist White people through both legal and extralegal means. Some were the targets of race riots and subsequently destroyed. One of the most famous examples is the bombing and razing of the all-Black Greenwood neighborhood of Tulsa, Oklahoma, in 1921 by the surrounding White community, which was jealous of its immense success.[3] At the time, Greenwood, known as "Black Wall Street," was the wealthiest Black community in America. This catastrophic event left 300 Blacks dead, 800 injured, 6,000 arrested and 10,000 homeless.[4] Unfortunately, this was far from an isolated incident.

Similar incidents occurred post-Reconstruction in thriving Black communities such as Atlanta, Georgia (1906), East St. Louis, Missouri (1917), Chicago, Illinois (1919), Washington, D.C. (1919), Knoxville, Tennessee (1919) and Rosewood, Florida (1923). Others became the involuntary sites of the local government projects with the construction of highways and railroads.[5] They became undiscoverable or, in some cases, practically uninhabitable.

Today, predominantly Black communities are shrinking or disappearing due to gentrification. Many that were not destroyed in the early 20th century have fallen into decline as a result of desegregation. Some scholars contend that Black business districts suffered once Black consumers were free to interact with the White market, which effectively multiplied the Black businesses' competition. The same issues ring true today, in spite of the recent resurgence of "Buy Black" as a result of the worldwide George Floyd, Breanna Taylor and Ahmaud Arbery protests.

Black Ownership Is Everything

Let's agree that thinking of ourselves as modern-day economic slaves is quite triggering. America is a capitalist society and, by and large, Blacks are not owners of much. This means White people *have more assets* (property, equities and businesses) and *employ* people with said assets to create more wealth.

Blacks are usually on the other side of the transaction. We are not significant owners of capital; we are owned by capital. Either you own or be owned. Wake up and realize that everything in America centers around ownership. Who owns what, drives our economy. While you might complain how rich you are making your boss – she is entitled to the profits because she owns the business. It's no secret that most wealth in America has been built through owning three things: property, equities and businesses, not cars, jewelry and clothes.

If you don't aspire to own these three things, then by default you aspire to be owned by the people who do. Either you own your home, or you pay rent to the person who does. Either you own a business, or you rely on the graciousness of the entrepreneur or the corporation to look out for your best interests. Either you own stocks and are invested in the market or you are being owned by potential inflation, wage stagnation and only one way to build wealth-saving your paycheck.

We can't pass down what we don't own. Passing down rent payments to the next generation is not the same as passing down the real estate for them to collect rents. Passing down a good word with the boss man to hire your child when he graduates college is not the same as passing down a business. Passing down what's left in your savings account is not the same as passing down an investment portfolio. Ownership is everything. Ownership is freedom. Ownership is American. Ownership must be more Black!

Until Los Angeles Lakers' LeBron James hit the scene, most professional basketball players had very little control over the team for which they played. Most players sat back and allowed their agents, owners, coaches or general managers to dictate what they could do on and off the court. It was LeBron who made bold moves to take control of what he owned: his brand and influence. He became the owner of multiple businesses, including an entertainment company and a foundation, all for the purpose of controlling his own destiny. He is not owned, he is owning.

The simple power of ownership is that it grants you more control and true economic freedom. You should aspire to control your own destiny. As I'm a little bit of a control freak, owning stuff works for me. If you are the same, then you should strive to *own more*. It's the only way you will get more control and freedom for yourself and your family.

Slavery is over, but ownership is not. Owners control the boards of every sector of the economy and non-owners are pawns. Adam Smith taught, capitalism is driven by the greed of owners of capital who deploy said capital to manufacture goods and services. By doing so, they use capital to hire people.

Net Worth Is More Important Than Net Pay

We need to take the concept of ownership more seriously.

This may sound simple, but it is very hard to make the behavioral switch from day-to-day to longer-term, owner-focused thinking.

Too many of us think net pay is more important than net worth. Where you work doesn't matter. How much you make

Being wealthy is not about how much you earn; it's about how much you're worth.

doesn't matter. How old you are doesn't matter. What matters is how much you own. Ownership offers the greatest potential for a better tomorrow.

Men lie, women lie, even churchgoers sometimes lie, but numbers don't. Personally, I'm a numbers-and-facts kind of guy, so I am going to emphasize a key number: Black people have over $1.3 trillion in spending power. That's more than some respected countries in this world spend. That, ladies and gentlemen, is Black ownership potential. Even so, Blacks are still financially far behind other ethnic groups in this country. One in five Black families have zero or negative net worth. According to an August 2019 article in the *New York Times*, the median family wealth for Black families is $17,600 compared to $171,000 for White families.[6] At the current rate of saving and wealth building in the Black community, it would take a Black family 225 years to catch up to the average White family. When compared to Asians, Whites, Hispanics and Native Americans, Blacks are in last place.

We're making money and clearly, we're spending money,

but most of us don't have any wealth because we don't own enough property, equities and businesses. I want to reemphasize – what you're earning in a paycheck and what you're worth are two vastly different concepts and ways of life. Don't dismiss this conversation because you earn over $75,000 a year because even so, you are more than likely to be under-invested in real estate, businesses and equities.

This isn't a "poor" Black folks' conversation. Yes, I know you might vacation at the Vineyard, but the truth is that you probably aren't "worth" what you show. Sometimes, we take a lot of pride in being part of an upper social class by *income,* but truth be told, if we really had it like that, we would be *passing down more* wealth than we do. So, please come off your high horse for a minute and be a part of the community conversation. You are not separate from "us."

To become owners, we must eradicate the take-home pay lifestyle. It's why white families hold the largest percentage of the national wealth.[7] They're making different financial decisions. Acknowledging the systematic reasons and failed public policy for Blacks won't change the number. White families are leaving their children the gift of ownership while, for the most part, we're passing down little to nothing.

We've been a net-income people and not net-worth people. We have been focused on the now and with little planning for the future. Net income people waste money on things that don't appreciate over time. Net income people don't put their money to work for them, they just spend it. Net income people aren't thinking about thriving, they're focused on and satisfied with surviving. Basically, Black people are still living for the moment with a "screw-the-future" mindset when it comes to generational wealth. We are stuck in a worry-about-today mode, while tomorrow is dominated by owners. This way of thinking is killing us and must end now!

If you know where your money is going to go before you get paid and it's not being put towards a long-term financial goal that includes ownership, then you're a net income person. If your focus is to just maintain, you're a net income person. If you don't understand the terms – net income, wealth building, investments, assets, liabilities, equity – then you're a net income person. You're working hard, but you don't have a lot to show for it. You're spending money on things that, at the end of the day, don't matter.

Net worth people educate themselves about money, how it moves, how to grow it and what to do with it. They invest as much of their money as they possibly can because they know investing their money is the best thing that they can do with it. They live within their means and don't overextend themselves using up credit and taking out loans for things they don't need.

If you're only concerned with how you're going to spend your take home pay, you're living in the past. That's money you've already earned and spent. Your financial future is the present. Your finances today reflect the decisions you made yesterday. If you want tomorrow to look like something, you must make the right decisions today. Make the decision to be an owner.

Ownership is a mentality. You need to think of long-term goals instead of instant gratification. Where do you want your life to be in 10 years? How are you going to get there? Will you still be living paycheck to paycheck, or will you be able to do what you want to do? Wealth accumulation is freedom to do what you want to do. I'm sorry, but net income thinking amounts to modern day economic slavery.

Why Own? Appreciation

Here is the secret of ownership...assets owned can appreciate and they can be passed down to the next generation. That is a clear distinction between just owning "stuff" and owning the "right stuff."

Stuff includes things like clothes, cars, boats, planes, certain jewelry, certain artwork, electronics, accessories or basically anything else that drops in value the minute you use it. We are spending our hard-earned cash on the wrong stuff; things with little to no value other than how they make us feel. Unfortunately, our "cool factor" sets trends for the masses in every area except owning real estate, businesses and portfolios.

It's time to flick a switch on our buying habits and start accumulating assets that appreciate most; things that have the potential to increase in value *after* we own them. This isn't rocket science, but I fear too many Black folks will read this and do nothing, so I am sounding the prophetic alarm to *know more, own more and pass down more!*

Ownership is what drives America. Those who accumulate the most appreciable assets have most of the power and influence. As Chris Rock once said in a concert, "Shaq is rich, but the guy who signs his check is wealthy!" Rock was alluding to the power of ownership over income. That's why Shaq now owns real estate, businesses and stocks! So, the question is–do you have an ownership mentality or not? Do you desire more freedom and control over your financial future? Are you willing to play the long game? Do you have what it takes to make the shift from living paycheck to paycheck toward living passive income to passive income?

Dear Black People, We Have a Support Issue!

When talking about increasing ownership in the Black community, all the possible obstacles must be acknowledged. And by obstacles, I don't mean just the external ones that we all know of, such as systematic and institutional racism. I want to point out the obstacles we can remove – those that might be accidentally cultural. Let's make the cultural shifts we need to get serious about Black ownership so that we're not left out in the future.

At a recent financial empowerment workshop for Black and Hispanic college-educated, dual-income, professional families, I posed the question "Why is it that people of color, particularly those in the Black and Latino communities, have significantly lower home ownership than Whites? Why don't we own as much property?" I asked this question in New

Jersey, where only 38% of Black households own property compared to nearly 60% of White households. It was a fair question since this ownership gap is one of the major drivers of the wealth gap in New Jersey, highlighting the difference between what people of color inherit versus Whites.

Here are two interesting responses raised by group members. They offer some insight into cultural issues that challenge our ownership potential. One response was from a young woman and Newark native who argued that the Black community's biggest problem was that it doesn't support its own. The community suffers from the proverbial "crabs-in-a-barrel" mentality best described by the phrase, "If I can't have it, neither can you." This is when the collective community becomes jealous or filled with a sense of self-loathing, so the members find a way to pull the success climber back down to the community's level. Her environment was rife with people who pulled each other down more than lifted each other up. As she began her ascent through college education and hard work, people within her sphere did not offer their support; they saw her as different.

We compete with one another in every aspect of life instead of helping to reach back and pull up our brethren so that they are also able to shine. This has to stop – now! There are enough assets, property and job growth for all of us if we just show one another how to attain them.

Another woman suggested that the Black community struggled with collaboration. Having grown up in a predominantly Jewish community, she witnessed how individuals collaborated in real estate projects and business ventures. She shared a story of how a property was purchased by three Jewish families who lived in her neighborhood. They weren't related, but they were able to pool their resources. Her question was, "Why don't we see more ventures into commercial real estate and otherwise in the Black community?" And she answered her own question by saying, "We don't collaborate as well."

Of course, there are many scholars who have investigated the issues concerning Black ownership, but I wanted to give you a peek into the thoughts of regular people. I acknowledge the above responses are just a small sample, but if we honor them, we can learn. Here's how I summarize both responses: Black America does not support its own as much as it could and suffers from the lack of collaboration. If this is true, then no wonder we own very little!

Most forms of ownership require exactly the two things mentioned above: support (financial, intellectual, legal) and collaboration (partnership and equity). It's easier to build together – as a couple, family or friend group – than it is to do so alone. Owners who collaborate with others increase their buying potential and spread their risk. Perhaps I can buy one property myself, but if I can collaborate with three other people with my means, we might be able to buy half a block!

There's a lot we can unpack here, but first, let's delve into the allegation that many in our community suffer from the crabs-in-the-barrel mentality. This basically means that the crabs are only concerned about getting themselves out of a barrel. Rather than supporting each other to climb out and escape the barrel one out at a time – the majority pulls down the highest crab as soon as it passes the others.

Let me be clear: I do not believe we can use a broad brushstroke to depict our whole community as suffering from this mentality, but I don't think there are enough of us who truly support beyond lip service. Ownership is all about support and collaboration. If we're going to really take on our culture and shift it, we must own that, as a collective, we don't support each other financially as much as we could. Or, in other words, we don't support each other in ownership as much as we support our own people when it comes to entertainment and amusement.

Hosting a party? Black folks show up. Beyoncé in concert? Black folks show up. A block party? Black folks show up. Cookout? Picnic? Family & Friends' day at the church? Black folks show up. But we've got to shift our attitudes from just supporting entertainment and amusement activities to supporting serious financial activities. The real issue is about building an attitude for Black support, otherwise we will only have a few who break through and many who stay behind. We will only have an uptick in supporting Black businesses as an emotional response to racism in America versus an intentional disruption of systematic racism.

How many times do you hear meaningful conversations in our community about ownership? The support issue is big – and it rears its ugly head in our spending. We don't spend our money primarily with Black-owned businesses, who then struggle to compete with better capitalized competitors.

Support is the basis for collaboration, but collaboration is the active duty of working together towards a specific aim or project. The best way to collaborate as owners is to pool our financial resources together. We do little in the way of collaboration because we have little in the way of support, and it's killing us. For example, why is it that other ethnic groups have arrived in America since 1980 in large numbers and have moved ahead of us? Because they collaborate better. These are the ethnic communities that comedians often tease in their routines because they own businesses. But the joke is on us, because those groups actually own the businesses!

For example, comedians often focus on the Indian American community for owning 7-Eleven stores. And while that stereotype may make for a humorous joke...it's a great stereotype to be associated with since 7-Eleven stores can be very profitable. Comedians make fun of the fact that Indians own businesses and that they're involved in franchising. Who teases Black America about ownership? No one! Moreover, I can't think of a single industry or type of business that is identified by the Black community...can you? While there are certainly a lot of Black-owned salons and barbershops, no one fully associates the ownership of these businesses exclusively with Black America.

I have a friend who owns a Subway franchise. In fact, he owns multiple Subway franchises. But he doesn't own them by himself: he is part of a family partnership. Each location is listed under a separate LLC and each LLC has close to 10 family member owners listed as partners. Since I am always interested in *knowing more*, I asked, "Why does your family own these franchises together as a business model?" He replied, "Because we left India poor, like most of us who arrive here. None of us came with enough money to buy a business on our own. In our culture, there are many ways in which we pool our money together to buy businesses and then we divide the profits." And I quote his most important phrase, "It's easier to build together than it is to build apart."

I'm not sharing this story with you to say Indians are better, that Jews are better, or that Koreans are better than us. They have their culture of money, and now we must subscribe to our own. Simply put, we can and will do better. God will bless us if we seek to *"possess the land"* that is before us.[8]

Move beyond the spirit of offense and see the real problem. Our business is already out in those streets. We have a proverbial sign hung around our necks that says, "We don't own enough." I'm not putting our business in the streets, but I'm challenging us to buy a piece of the street and place a business on it! Playtime is over.

Family, ownership is a mentality. So, before you jump in asking, "Tell me how to own stuff" and "What is the best stuff to own?" slow down and receive the message. Ownership requires support and collaboration. There are plenty of great books written by experts on how to get there and the top ten steps to success...but we have greater issues. They are billowing underneath the surface, and they're insidious. We need a kind of deliverance. I would argue that support and collaboration are the best ways for us to get ahead as a family, friend group or community.

There Is Power in Our Pooled Dollars

There is an overwhelming sense that Black history is attributable to those who thought about our future – especially our economic future. Martin Luther King, Jr., Marcus Garvey, Malcolm X, Ida B. Wells and other historical leaders understood and demonstrated *the culture of money*. These leaders worked tirelessly for Blacks to have free access to markets and opportunities. They understood the power a dollar wields, especially when pooled together.

Everything they did was not necessarily for the moment, but for the next generation. It's almost like Dr. King was from the future—knowing that if things did not change, wealth gaps would be created, and Black people would be on the wrong side. So, he urged us to work together to get ahead.

Your one dollar doesn't seem like much until you realize the power unlocked when you agree to pool your dollars with others. This is exactly what happened during the bus boycotts in the 60s. The aggregate power of Black people agreeing to spend their individual dollars (or hold them back) the same way would get better results.

When we boycotted the buses, it crippled the local economies of cities across America. When we boycotted stores, they had to change their discriminatory behaviors. *The culture of money* is about understanding the value and power of each dollar. It's also about how putting dollars together creates more gain and less pain in almost every area of your life.

Say it with me, "Dollars together matter more than dollars apart." Confess it until you believe it. Our dollars together can cause an increase. This is a fundamental principle. Your dollar has power, but our dollars have more power – to buy, own and invest. If we don't intentionally use our dollar power, we are unintentionally abusing it. We should invest in things that secure our community, employ our people and build our wealth.

> If used right today, our money has the potential to shift us into a whole new tomorrow.

As I said previously, the economic impact of our dollars is greater than we can possibly imagine.

Property Ownership Closes the Gap

Why would you not want to own real estate when over the past 200 years, roughly 90% of the world's millionaires have been created by investing in real estate![9]

For the average person, real estate offers the best way to develop significant wealth. If freed slaves could see the value of buying land and figure it out, so can you. As you will hear me repeat, you don't need money to get rich; you need time and patience! For any form of investing, its best to get started early with real estate so you can put time on your side. If you are in your 20s, don't listen to your friends who will tell you owning a home is too much responsibility. Get out of your parents' house and own your own.

One of the best ways to take on an ownership mentality is to buy your first primary residence. This is wisdom that still works. They aren't making more land, so eventually it will always cost more.

I asked a friend what financial advice his grandparents gave to him. He told me what Essie Brown, his grandmother, used to say: "When you have property within the family, it always continues to have value. Don't look at property as if you're always going to build something on it. Look at it as something that can be used to build the future."

I know there are many sophisticated arguments and models that argue against homeownership. But as far as I'm concerned, the numbers don't lie; owning real estate is the #1 way to build wealth and *pass down more.*

Don't believe me? Consider that today, the five largest White landowners *own more* land than all Black people combined: over 9 million acres.[10] According to *Business Insider*, April 2019,[11] they are: telecommunications giant, John Malone (2.2 million acres), media mogul, Ted Turner (2 million acres), forest products producers, The Emmerson Family (1.9 million acres) and The Reed Family (1.7 million acres), and sports mogul and St. Louis Rams owner, Stan Kroenke (1.4 million acres). Ted Turner owns as much land by himself as roughly 25% of land Black people own collectively.

We don't buy land, we rent it. Then we leave this world

with nothing to pass on to the next generation. Real estate investing can give you a tangible investment that will appreciate over time. It has the potential to generate income on a monthly basis and you can pass it on to the next generation. More than 70% of White families own their homes and they're passing down that real estate to their children as their property continues to appreciate with value.

There's open discussion on the clear connection between the wealth gap and housing inequality. New research by macroeconomist Matthew Rognlie[12] found that housing inequality (that is, how much more expensive some houses are than others) is the key factor in rising wealth. His research shows that the percentage of wealth from real estate ownership has grown significantly since around 1950. It has grown substantially more than other forms of capital such as business ownership and equities.

When you look back, some of the folk wisdom we were taught as a community was shrewd financial genius. The challenge before us is to get back to this kind of ownership mentality and *own more*. We have access to better education and income opportunities than our ancestors did. So, if we honor and carry forward the same value, to *own more*, then we can achieve more than they did. This is exactly why they told us to *own more*; they wanted us to surpass their wealth.

Despite widespread, legal housing discrimination in the 1950s and 1960s, the number of Black households that owned their own homes increased 20% from 1950 to 1970, but somehow since the passing of the Fair Housing Act in

1968 the Black homeownership rate has not increased. This is called the Black Homeownership Paradox.[13] There are many theories, including the damaging effects of redlining and predatory lending post 1968, but those theories don't address the fact that there has been substantial progress in educational attainment, accompanied by increased wages, incomes, wealth and health since 1968. So, can we blame 100% of the lack of increase in ownership on redlining and predatory lending? No, that would not be keeping it 100! There is room for us to improve.

While most of us can brag that we make more money than our ancestors ever did, few of us *own more* than they did. They had different money values. *The culture of money* reconnects us to these values so that we can live the dream they saw for us.

When you get your ducks in a row and purchase a house, don't buy too much house. You don't have to be "house poor" to make the investment work for you. According to Investopedia, being house poor means a person spends a large proportion of his total income on home ownership, including mortgage payments, property taxes, maintenance and utilities. House poor individuals are short of cash for discretionary items and tend to have trouble meeting other financial obligations.

You need to purchase well within your means of financial operation. Ideally, you want to spend somewhere around 30% of your income on your mortgage. Spending 40% is pushing it but could work depending on other aspects of your financial situation. If you invest more than 50% of your income on a house, you are most definitely spending too much.

Buying a multi-family unit is a better idea. You can purchase a duplex or a two-family flat and let your tenants pay your mortgage. Can you imagine how much income you could free up if somebody else was paying your mortgage? If you took that money and invested it, imagine how much further ahead you'd be in life in a year or so.

The longer you own a home and/or a rental property, the more equity you build. According to NerdWallet, home equity is the current market value of your home, minus what you owe. Any gain comes from paying down the principal balance on your loan or an increase in market value over time. Equity is an asset and is considered part of your net worth.

Just because you have bought a house doesn't mean you're done investing. The mindset of building wealth should be a permanent change in lifestyle. Keep in mind that you still need to be able to make financial moves after you buy the house. Persistence and relentlessness are your new norm.

Remember, we desire financial education so that we can increase our financial confidence and capability, live by a plan, execute it and repeat. *Knowing more* allows us to *own more* appreciable assets.

Ownership supports positive identity development and increases our self-esteem. Owners are more optimistic about the future. They dream a lot because what is owned can be developed and leveraged to *own more*. As an owner, you should be constantly thinking about the future and the money moves it will take today to make the future a reality.

Unlock the Power of Ownership Circles

Jean, a member of my church, has been selling real estate for 30 years. She works in a New Jersey mixed suburb where she told me it is not unusual for her to sell real estate to ethnic circles of people who pool their money together to buy property. She specifically identified certain Central Americans, Asians and African groups that pool their resources to buy and share a single home as a means for everybody to have a place to start from. Years later, as they work and build their lives in America, these groups continue to pool their resources to buy more property, with some of the family going to live in the second property. Jean said that after ten or fifteen years, she has helped these groups build substantial portfolios of property because they collaborate and pool their dollars together for ownership.

What is holding you back from pooling your financial resources with other families or friends to buy property or start a business? I do enough speaking and teaching on this topic to know that most Black people will say, "Amen. Mm-hmm (affirmative)," to the concept of working together in any capacity. Yet, those same people will not move into action.

One of the things that we could do better is think more broadly and seek opportunities for ownership circles. Your circle could include family, friends, church members or business associates. Ownership circles are based upon the pooling of resources because pooled money can definitely work harder than just your money alone. It's time to work together, not apart. Family, church-wide and community-wide ownership circles are *the culture of money*.

Minneapolis Somalians are *the culture of money*. A company called Star Finance is working to solve the issue for the Somalian community concerning the often-unaffordable cost of a mortgage in the city. In most cases, Somalians come to America often with very little education and very little money. They are a hardworking people, but as immigrants they have no credit history and background. This allows lenders to have a legitimate basis for declining their loan applications.

The leaders of the Somalian community explored the potential of collective wealth and came up with a group ownership plan. The result was Star Finance, a culturally appropriate, non-predatory mortgage option designed specifically for Somali immigrants and without the need of a bank. Star Finance's mortgage model cuts out banks and middlemen. It's based on the simple premise of recruiting 200 Somalis to each invest $2,500 to buy four homes in the city. Prospective homeowners rent the houses to own from Star Finance. The current plan is for Star to be a for-profit limited liability company (LLC). It will be majority owned by a Somali community-based, non-profit, which gets at least 51% of the profits from the mortgages. It's a wonderful model which needs to be unpacked and explored more, because this is a model that churches, nonprofits and even families can follow.

While we didn't have a model or name for it, my siblings and I lived *the culture of money* and pooled resources for property ownership. Pooling our resources never meant managing each other's money, but it has meant accessing each other's funds to open businesses and buy homes.

Terri and I were able to transfer the equity we had built up in a home to my mother. Our family was growing so we moved to a larger home. Our original house was in great condition in a nice neighborhood, so my mother assumed the mortgage and inherited all the equity we had built in the property.

We also contributed to the down payment of my oldest sister's first house. My younger sister has also presented me with opportunities to pool our resources for a property in New York City, when the right opportunity presents itself.

What I'm speaking about is my family's subculture and values. The Salters look out for each other. We don't help each other for the purpose of getting or sharing equity. We've pooled resources to help each other get ahead. As each of us has achieved success, we maintain a sense of responsibility to support and collaborate with each other. These are facts.

I'm most proud of my sisters. They are powerful, awesome Black women who have taught me so many wonderful lessons. Over the years, we have pooled resources to buy each other cars, houses and even pay for education expenses. While we may not be in each other's lives every day, we have taken a communal approach to getting our family from financial struggle to financial peace. I can't recall a time when we knowingly or intentionally forfeited the opportunity to support and collaborate. The only times we struggled alone is when we withheld our struggle from each other. Honestly, I probably could have avoided my bankruptcy if I shared my financial troubles with my sisters. They would have scraped up all the money they had to help me pay off all my bills to avoid it. But my own pride, embarrassment and shame caused me to hide my situation from them. So, I walked that path alone, because I wanted to. Those emotions and behaviors are what got in my way.

I know we are not the only Black family conditioned to help each other. There are many stories of like-minded families that have learned the secrets of pooling money, support and collaboration. We need these stories to expand the theory of collaboration so it becomes a part of Black culture. This is the issue of our day. If we don't get serious about ownership, we're going to be left behind.

What would happen if every person who reads this called a family or friends meeting and began to pool money together for creating an investment club, investing in a business or property? We would change the narrative greatly. Maybe it can't happen within your family circle, but what about your friend or business associate circles? What has gotten in *your* way to stop you from trying out this option?

The finances of the circle must be managed by the most knowledgeable and trustworthy person. If no one has the financial capability, keep saving together and choose one person in the circle who is trustworthy to *know more*. For example, to buy a property together, you need a person to collect the money, deposit it in the bank and provide monthly accountability to others in the circle. You can also outsource that expertise. It's better to pay for knowledge than pay the price for moving forward without it.

Depending on your family or friend dynamics, whenever pooling money together, I highly urge you to keep it as business and draft legal paperwork. Everyone involved should agree on the submitted terms, so there will be no reason to disagree later.

Star Finance is a great testimony to what Black people can do if we work together. We can buy homes to share, strip malls, multi-tenant properties and more if we unlock the power of pooling.

Owning Black Businesses Closes The Wealth Gap Faster

There are over 11 million millionaires in America and most of them did not inherit wealth; they built it from scratch.[14] One study shows that business ownership is the greatest equalizer in wealth disparity, reducing the average wealth gap from a multiplier of 13 to three. Let me break this down for you. In 2014, the median net worth of non-Hispanic White households was $130,800. The median net worth of Black households was $9,590. This simply means White households have a net worth that is 13.5 times Black households. But owning a business can dramatically and quickly reduce that gap. This means the numbers would look more like $130,800 for White households and $43,600 if members of the Black community owned more businesses. We would not be on par with other ethnic groups, but in a much better place.

Another way of looking at this data is to see that owning a business can increase Black family wealth by 4.5 times. We need to get in on this action and I'll share why. Owning property is one thing, but owning a business is another. Blacks need to *own more* businesses because it has the potential to increase net worth by 13 times. While we have many individual success stories, we need more ownership.

Regardless of how you feel about him, Jay-Z didn't become the first hip hop billionaire from rapping. He might have started

> **Business ownership is the best way to turbo charge your wealth exponentially.**

off with rapping, but then he developed an impressive business ownership collection–including a clothing line, several brands of alcohol, sports management services and music streaming services to name a few. Many Black moguls in entertainment are following his pattern of investing in businesses. For instance, Jay-Z's protégé, Nas, is part of a really dope investment team, QueensBridge Venture Partners out of Harlem, that has made some impressive moves like investing in Dropbox, Lyft, Casper and Robin Hood.

Why do you think these artists have been drawn into

becoming business owners? They don't want to be owned; they want to be owners. They've come to understand that ownership is the only way to get freedom in a capitalist society. I'm sure they have plenty of war stories about being taken advantage of when they were simply artists relying upon the good graces of others for their income. Now that they are in control, not only are they making more income, they are using it right to create businesses.

Provide More Black Support

I know you've heard something like this before: a dollar circulates for only six hours in the Black community. Here's the issue: a dollar circulates for 17, 20 and 30 days in the White, Jewish and Asian communities, respectively. Please don't read past the underlying meaning: the numbers simply mean that members of other communities support their businesses more than we do.

Listen, I know the struggle is real, and that the Black community is fighting uphill against a litany of issues. Racism has done a really good job of setting Blacks back. It can be exhausting and debilitating and cause us to focus on our own chapter and miss the larger narrative.

In capitalist America, the spirit of community support is what causes some groups to prosper more than others. Want to start a business? You need support. As your enterprise grows, you're going to need employees to support your vision.

Unfortunately, in the Black community we often wait

until somebody's made it before we offer our support. In other words, we put our celebrities on pedestals. They get our undying, unwavering support. I'm glad they do because otherwise they'd have limited careers playing slaves, housekeepers and singing only "Black music." Meanwhile, there are local Black heroes, innovators and businesspeople who only get the support of dollars that circulate within the Black community for six measly hours!

Before you disagree, remember the numbers don't lie. Remember, we have $1.3 trillion in buying power and most of the products we buy are not produced within the Black community. The "Buy Black," slogan is proof that we don't support Black! We shouldn't have to say, "Buy Black"! Shouldn't it be intrinsic? I have yet to see "Buy Asian" or "Buy Jewish" ads running. Why? They don't have to because within those communities providing support is well understood and second nature.

Have you not noticed the trend of independently owned Asian supermarkets popping up all over the country? Look back 20 years and you rarely saw one. And, where are they? In communities where other Asians live. Asians know that the products they want aren't found at ShopRite, Kroger or Publix. So rather than spend all their dollars at those stores, they've agreed to import those products, and put them all under one roof where Asians can shop. This is how they keep a dollar in their community for 30 days.

This business model is successful because Asian entrepreneurs know the Asian community will prioritize spending their dollars at the Asian supermarket rather than at the main brand markets. That's not a racial statement: it's a fact. Since those dollars are spent with an Asian business owner, they help further develop the business and perpetuate the business plan within the Asian community. And it all comes down to one word: support.

There are many other ethnic communities where we can find these trails of support, but not as much as we should in the Black communities. Who we support needs to change. Spend less time supporting changeable celebrities like R. Kelly and more time supporting Black ownership.

We are failing the Golden Rule[15] when we don't support Black ownership. Let me be both clear and realistic – we live in a global economy – so it's impossible to support only Black ownership. But we can be more intentional and prioritize our support. *The culture of money* **supports Black ownership in all forms. We put our dollars where Black owners have taken risk.**

I do see a modicum of support through nonprofit programs, Black business days or other initiatives. And yes, there are enclaves and community pockets where awareness and support are big issues getting a lot of play. But geographically there is variance. Harlem and Atlanta may offer more supportive environments than Boston or Gary. What I'm speaking about is Black culture. We need to show the same support to the Black construction company as we do to Tyler Perry.

Provide More Support To Black Women

We have an incredible opportunity to invest in our college grads who are incredibly smart. Over the past five years, Black women have led the charge and unprecedented numbers of them have started businesses. In fact, according to the most recent annual State of Women-Owned Businesses Report, commissioned by American Express, women of color represent 39% of the total female population in the U.S. but account for 89% of the net new women-owned businesses per day (1,625) over the past year. Black women are killing it.[16]

While the number of women-owned businesses grew 21% from 2014 to 2019, firms owned by women of color grew an astounding 43% and Black women-owned firms grew even faster at 50%. Black women-owned businesses represented the highest rate of growth of any group in the number of firms between 2014 and 2019, as well as between 2018 and 2019. They started 42% of net new women-owned businesses, which is three times their share of the female population (14%). At the end of the day, Black female-owned businesses need our support, which in this context, looks like intentionally driving your dollars to these vendors of goods and services.

Some main reasons all Black businesses need more support are their limited access to credit, their lack of social capital and lack of connections to garner investments. These issues make it more difficult to gain traction than their better-capitalized competition.

It's well documented that not only are Black homeowners

red-lined, so are Black businesses. Redlined means there are banks that have systematically drawn red lines around entire communities of people that they deem high risk. Banks will then do one of two things: avoid lending to people within those communities or lend capital at terms that are completely exorbitant. In fact, the Community Reinvestment Act (CRA) was a federal law enacted in 1977 to force banks to lend to minority communities. It encourages depository institutions to meet the credit needs of low and moderate income neighborhoods. The CRA requires federal regulators to assess how well each bank fulfills its obligations to these communities. The CRA has done some tremendous things, but it's not enough.

When you look at Wall Street and the world of private equity, it's also no secret that very little private equity goes to Black founders and Black start-up geniuses. A study by the National Community Reinvestment Coalition proves that Black and Hispanic men seeking small business loans face stricter underwriting guidelines and worse treatment from bank officers than less qualified White men.[17] Minorities face treatment that discourages applying for business loans. Many would-be entrepreneurs' dreams die due to a lack of access to credit. The money circles discussed earlier can be a solution to this problem as well.

Likewise, the social circles of many Blacks do not include large groups of people familiar with risk taking and investing in start-ups. Even the most educated among us struggle to find venture capital for their start up ideas. On the other hand, you often hear the stories from White entrepreneurs speaking of family and friends investing capital in their start-ups. This is significant because if a White entrepreneur gets declined (which, according to statistics, is less likely), he can probably go to family members and family friends to ask for start-up capital. Meanwhile, most brothers or sisters will have to start with faith and whatever they might have in their bank accounts.

I hope you see how this might play out in the marketplace. One business starts with a better capital base than the other. More capital means more potential for better staff, more product on the shelves, more marketing to reach customers—just more. So, before you complain that the Black business owner has less on the shelf, understand that the system is set up to ensure that happens. We ought to celebrate any Black business that gets to market with any product considering this scenario.

Let's not forget that Black women are starting and growing businesses at record rates. They need our dollars because they are striving for excellence. *The culture of money* is driven by a team of powerful Black women. This movement, like many Black movements, gains its momentum from the work of dedicated and educated sisters. That is not by accident, it is by design. Where I can balance the scales with my dollars, I certainly will. I hope you do the same.

My Personal Rude Awakening

Part of my culture of money journey included navigating past many of the obstacles I listed above. When I started my company Professional Risk Solutions in 2001, every bank that I applied to denied my loan. My credit score was roughly 710, my debt to income ratio 24%, I had savings to invest in my start-up. I was a college-educated, senior vice president of a publicly traded company and I was starting a business where I had contacts, credibility and expertise. Still, I didn't get a single approval.

So, like most Black business dreamers, I took a calculated risk and stepped out on faith, using my savings and all my credit cards to launch the business in my home. Meanwhile, a White peer in the industry started a competing company with a $25 million investment from a private equity firm. I had to compete against billion-dollar companies and well-capitalized new entrants with only the money in my bank account, credit cards and Jesus! Good thing that faith and good works are profitable: my company still exists nearly 20 years later!

Please don't overlook the struggle of Black business owners. I was facing an uphill battle in quicksand. Without some divine intervention, like gospel singer Marvin Sapp said, "I never would have made it!"

Here's another issue we need to address more intimately: Black dreamers need Black dollars to earn more than any other ethnic group. As a new insurance brokerage, my first goal was to be the preferred provider of commercial and executive liability insurance to minority-owned businesses. Unfortunately, I quickly discovered that just because I was Black wasn't enough to get other successful Black businesses to engage my company.

My heart was often disappointed by the Black executives in positions of power and the Black owners who did not give me a shot. The truth was, I had to readjust my business plan to compete with the White guys for White guys' business. Sadly, it was easier for me to build a clientele reaching White customers than Black ones. It hasn't remained that way, but early on that certainly was the case. I did not feel the support of the community as a Black professional in terms of new contracts and dollars, though I did garner community support for my position as a role model. And I'm not the only one. Over the years, many Black business owners have voiced the same complaint.

It is sad to think that if we don't step up to support our own, White companies will continue to "discover" Black consumers and drive Black businesses to extinction using their "better" capital base to win the lion's share of the market. We can't allow this to happen.

Creating Black wealth through entrepreneurship is the culture of money. Risk takers should be rewarded with our dollars.

I'm not arguing that you should only support Black businesses, which would be nearly impossible to do. But we have to be more intentional in helping our brothers and sisters.

If the banks and Wall Street won't support us, then we should be able to rely on our own community members to spend their dollars with us so that we can grow, hire better staff, add more products/services and just do better.

We can control our own destiny. My bias is clear: if you have a chance to start a business, do so. But not everybody needs to start a business. Take a good look at yourself to understand who you are and your capabilities. For example, some people are better wired to be the maverick and start something new. Some are better at investing dollars with those mavericks. Still others may not do either but will be determined to support those mavericks as a customer.

My personal path was not a direct shot to entrepreneurism. I spent 10 years in Corporate America where I gained polish, professionalism and skills before starting my first business. My career as an underwriter at Chubb Insurance Company prepared me to be a better entrepreneur. I learned how to carry myself in a way that garnered respect and build credibility. I also learned how to communicate more clearly and to be a strategic thinker. Because of my background, I needed that exposure to Corporate America, and you might need it, too.

I think it's a great strategy to intentionally spend three to five years working in Corporate America after college. You'll learn how to be professional, show up to work on time, write a business memo, deal with customers and vendors, sell and work with employees and teammates. Why not gather all that intel before you launch into our own venture?

Mavericks are wired differently. I know many of them who have been wildly successful, but the corporate environment didn't work for their personality type. In fact, because of their wiring, they are often misunderstood and feel displaced in Corporate America. They are often combative because they challenge the work process in a place where everyone is conditioned to think the same thoughts.

Mavericks need to control their own destiny. I was not a maverick, but I grew into one. I had to learn how to be more charismatic so I could attract more customers and investors to my ideas. If you already have the money, social network and clientele, then perhaps there's no need to take the corporate path.

If you don't have the appetite for risk, then don't quit your day job. Perhaps you might be the type to start a side hustle so you can earn more money. This is my infamous description of side hustle: "Work a 9 to 5 day and a 5 to 9 night," so you still have enough time to have family dinner, read a book, pray, go to sleep and repeat. Entrepreneurs usually must sacrifice many of those things, but side hustlers have a little more wiggle room with their time at home.

My overall message is simple. Start, invest in, or buy from Black businesses.

Franchise Systems Could be the Way

Just as a family can start an investment club or pool its money to buy a home, we can model other successful communities that buy businesses. We can and should more proactively pool our resources to own businesses, especially franchise systems. McDonald's has one of the most diverse franchise systems. Black franchise owners showing up as some of the wealthiest Black families in America. Many of them are now second-generation franchise owners with second-generation wealth.

Pooling money to start a franchise is great for those who want to skip the corporate experience, are new college grads or don't want to learn from the school of hard knocks. Franchises can be less risky, depending on the franchisor. Black America should attack the franchise market. The beauty of franchising is that it gives you the opportunity to basically get a business education on the job.

Equity Investments Build Wealth without Work

The best way to get your "money making money" while you sleep is to invest in the stock market. The beauty of the market is that you can own a slice of a business without having to work. Perhaps not everyone can be an entrepreneur, but anyone can be a partial business owner. The easiest way to own a piece of a business is to buy stock in one. You can buy a stock of an individual company or buy shares of a mutual fund, which will invest your dollars for you in various companies, private or public. **Owning stocks is business ownership.** When you buy an individual stock, or a share of a mutual fund, you legally become an owner of the entities in which you invest. Your ownership rights include the right to vote as a shareholder at annual meetings, even if you only own one share. You don't have to be adept at entrepreneurship to commit to owning stocks in businesses.

Family, we need to *own more* than real estate – we need to be in the market. Fundamentally, you want to be able to buy shares low and sell high over a long period of time. Buying low and selling high is purchasing something at a value, holding on to it *for a while* and selling when it's worth more than what you paid for it. Examples of buying low and selling high include: buying a house for $150,000 and selling it for $200,000; selling a domain name after making it popular on Google for more than what you purchased it for; or buying a website, building it up and selling it after you enhance it to the max. You need to invest in learning how to buy low and sell high to reap the benefits of asset appreciation. No matter what the investment is, buying low and selling high is the essence of investment and wealth building.

Investments put your money to work for you and like real estate and business ownership, they can create another stream of income and wealth. You can take one stream of income (your paycheck) and turn it into several investment streams through ownership. Here's the cheat code to investment: you don't need a lot of money to build a stock market portfolio. You need time and consistency.

Investing in the Stock Market Also Closes the Gap

Owning a portfolio is the tried-and-true method of wealth

builders that helped create the wealth gap in the first place. Self-made millionaires' top sources of assets include investments/capital appreciation, compensation and employee stock options and profit sharing. Individuals with inherited wealth usually use their head start in life to build even more wealth by investing in businesses and real estate as asset sources. In short, when it comes to owning portfolios, the self-made are more likely to add equity investments and the trust fund babies are more likely to own real estate portfolios. Most studies show that wealthy people are mainly concerned with preserving wealth. They see owning real estate, businesses and stocks as the best way to maintain or grow wealth.

You don't have to be super rich or super connected to invest in the market. Ronald Reed was a janitor who died a multimillionaire at the age of 92. This man worked as a janitor his entire life until the day he died. He donated $8 million to various charities. How can a man who lived his entire life working in arguably one of the lowest positions in American society accumulate a multimillion-dollar fortune without anyone noticing?

In his spare time, he learned to invest. He learned the importance of building wealth, and he made it happen. If you're reading this, you probably earn more money at your job than that man did. I bet when he started working, he was paid a small wage that would make you cuss somebody out if it was offered to you...yet he died a multimillionaire.

A secretary named Sylvia Bloom died a multimillionaire

and donated her fortune of $8.2 million as well. She worked until she was 96 years old and accumulated a serious amount of wealth. A teacher named Margaret Southern did the same thing and donated $8.4 million after her death.

So, a janitor, a secretary and a teacher who worked regular jobs managed to become multimillionaires during their lifetimes. These people didn't have financial backgrounds. Only one had a formal education, and she was a teacher. They got off work and invested in themselves by taking the time to understand how money works and then invested in their futures.

They didn't drive new cars; they didn't stop working; and they didn't make any noticeable changes as they accumulated wealth. They stuck to the script until the day they died. The people in all three examples mentioned were White. I mentioned them because I could not easily find stories of Black individuals to match.

To put this idea of accumulating wealth into perspective even further, the average college bachelor's degree holder makes a total of $1.2 million over the course of his entire working career. If you live modestly, you could earn enough to take care of yourself, but do you want to just survive, or do you want to thrive and have more than a little something? Just earning a paycheck from your job isn't going to cut it. You don't have any legitimate excuses to not accumulate wealth.

We need more stories like Damon Williams, a pre-teen brother from Chicago who took the little money he had to invest in Nike and Adidas, the companies we traditionally give our money to by purchasing their products. This kid had a mature, diverse investment portfolio that was worth $50,000 by the time he was 14 years old.

He was not one of those kids who played the violin at three years old or finished college at age 12. He was obviously intelligent, but the biggest difference between him and the rest of the kids his age was the way he viewed money and its role in his life. He understood the idea of wealth building and long-term goal planning. At 14 years old, he was a wealth-minded individual and had been investing in his wealth since he was six years old! Imagine where you could be with just a few years of investment dedication.

Meanwhile, Donald Trump inherited a successful family business from his dad and filed six bankruptcies in 18 years. All he had to do is maintain his wealth, yet he dropped the ball repeatedly. He has lost billions of his own money and assets on top of other people's money and assets. He's been sued throughout his career and since he's been President.

Wealth-minded people put their money to work. To them, money is an employee and a tool for investing. They make their money get a job. Wealth-minded people plan and focus on long-term financial goals. Their net income, which is today's wealth, in later years is called delayed gratification.

Consistency and Time Are Wealth Cheat-Codes

Usually during my financial education workshops, people ask me what they should invest in. My first problem with their question is that before you choose what to invest in, you need to make sure that you even have the capability to invest. You need to be able to regularly contribute capital from savings to an investment account so you're consistently and continually making buys in the market and building a portfolio over the longest time period possible. Here's why: the rock layer of investing is consistency and time. You can't be successful implementing one without the other; you must do both at the same time. As I mentioned before, the historical rate of return in the market is roughly 7%. So, the only thing you need to do to earn that average is invest long enough through the market's downturns and upturns to experience that 7% gain or better.

After the 2008 Great Recession, the market went on a tremendous bull run (which means stocks gain at least 20% from their most recent low) creating massive amounts of wealth, mainly for White people. No matter when this run ends, the recovery from the Great Recession is already the longest bull market in American history. Spanning more than a decade, the market boom has been driven by a combination of slow-but-steady economic growth, record corporate profits and record low interest rates. This bull market has created massive amounts of wealth for investors in the know. Very little of this wealth has been funneled into the Black community.

Another important rule of investing—don't invest money you're going to need in the near term. Covid-19 has stretched the definition of near term to mean 18-24 months!

Investments should only be made from your excess or abundance. Use your savings to invest. The first rules of investment – consistency and time – will be violated if you have not first established savings. You won't be able to invest consistently because it will take only one cash emergency for you to pull your money out of the market. And by pulling your money out of the market, you'll lose out on any potential gains.

Here are a couple of examples about time and consistency:

- If you invested $1,000 in Coca-Cola ten years ago, you'd have $2,800 today, almost tripling your wealth
- If you invested $1,000 in Apple, instead of buying the company's overpriced products, you'd have $13,000 today. That's 13 times increase in wealth
- If you invested $1,000 in Tesla, you'd have $22,327. That's 22 times your wealth

I hope you get the picture on what you may be missing. You can't triple your wealth by increasing your salary, but you can do it by owning property, stocks and/or a business.

Buy Stock Before You Buy Product

Here's a little behind-the-scenes investment secret. I tracked Tesla stock after its initial public offering (IPO) and I have followed the company's founder Elon Musk since he was one of the founders of PayPal. I knew he was onto something with Tesla. The company and its products had the cool factor and seemed poised to become the Apple of cars if it could produce enough vehicles to match the demand.

Since Musk was a serial entrepreneur, it was clear to me that he could raise money if the company ran into trouble. In addition, he was a billionaire and had enough money to recapitalize if needed. So, I took a risk and invested in Tesla stock after its IPO settled. I was able to buy the stock at price below $30 bucks a share. Eventually the company took off as Tesla became a household brand. I watched the stock rise to $50, then $100, then $200 and beyond. I sold some of my shares at a very high price compared to what I paid for each and bought a Tesla. Don't miss that comment: in other words, I let Tesla buy me a Tesla. It was a "treat me" moment, (yep, my Money Reparations script was in full throttle).

A critical financial planner might argue I should not have taken money out of the market to buy a car, overlooking the fact that investors routinely take profits. Trust me, wealthy investors use proceeds to buy all kinds of assets. I want to make it very clear that I do not ascribe to the "deny yourself everything" philosophy, especially for people who have been denied so much in society. We need to "treat ourselves" every now and then. However, the big issue for us is to make sure we can afford our lifestyle and learn to let Tesla buy us Teslas and let Apple buy us iPhones versus the other way around!

Here's why the amount of time you keep your money in the market is such a major factor: compound interest will make your investment grow at a faster rate than simple interest (like when you keep your cash in a savings account). Compound interest essentially means earning interest on the interest that gets reinvested over time. Most of us are losing sleep thinking about how to make money while it should be the opposite.

Black people are not taking advantage of compounding; the power of letting your money make you money while you sleep. Most of us are losing sleep trying to think about how to make money. Any reasonably intelligent person can see why one of the richest men in the world (at over $60 billion), Warren Buffett, is committed to the equity market. One of his most famous quotes is, "My wealth has come from a combination of living in America, lucky genes and compound interest." So, the question becomes, "What is holding you back from consistency and time?" Why are you afraid to take risk?

The stock market is not like the pyramid schemes that we often see running through our communities. Pyramid schemes are deceitful and illegal systems of making money based on recruiting an ever-increasing number of unsuspecting "investors." Usually, they fall apart and everyone ends up losing their money to the crook who started the pyramid scheme. This is not good stewardship.

Start a Family Investment Club

Kevon Chisolm was my roommate at Drew University. As an economics major, he was always interested in the stock market and how it worked. I often saw him perusing the *Wall Street Journal* and staying abreast of what was going on, even though, like me, he had no money to invest as a college student. After graduation he received his master's degree in African American Studies at Yale, and eventually settled into a career as a federal trademark attorney. While he has made a lot of nice moves throughout his career, the most brilliant move he made was to start an investment club with his family.

He now runs TheBlackWallStreeter.com (which explains the how and why of starting an investment club). His story and pattern are *the culture of money*. Kevon's investment circle included his wife, mother, mother-in-law, father-in-law and uncle. They started with monthly meetings focused on financial education and learning how to invest in the market together.

Early on, they leaned on Kevon's knowledge, but he urged them all to understand the importance of financial education. The club model was simple: each person learned how to research and recommend stocks to the group, the group voted on which stocks to choose and then they invested money they had saved. The power of pooling worked to their advantage since none of them had enough money individually to build a substantial portfolio.

After doing this for many years and remaining disciplined, at the height of their club's actions they accumulated hundreds of thousands in their portfolio. That is what I call real wealth! None of the club members were making six-figure salaries at the time, but together with pooled resources they created wealth faster.

As far as I know, the Chisolm Family investment club is one of the longest running Black family investment clubs in the country. They've been investing together for over 20 years. Once again, you can see the principles of support, collaboration and partnership.

Black people need to understand the power of a circle. Like the Star Finance model for property ownership in Minneapolis, the investment club model is readily available for families, friend groups and church groups to take advantage of. The investment club model, when done correctly, forces every individual to *know more*. It forces savings. It forces a certain fiscal discipline.

> Ownership is easier, faster and less risky when its shared.

The Goal Is Do It Together

The goal here is that we will work together by investing more together. The Chisolm investment club is the circle model; Star Finance is the real estate model. Every investment Terri and I have ever made, we've made it together. In fact, while I may be the financial guru of the family, Terri has great discernment and incredible sensibilities. She is probably the better steward and budgeter between us. So, if you put those skills together, we have a healthy balance of risk and reward.

There are all sorts of resources and websites where you can find out more about how to start an investment club within your own family, community or church group. Let's build wealth together, faster, because we don't have the luxury of doing it one by one. We need to do this community wide. Take the blueprint and run with it. I'm laying it out for you. How each of you work this in your own community or family is going to be up to you.

That's what *the culture of money* is; a set of ideas and a framework for you to interpret. Maybe you don't have enough family members who have the vision, the foresight, the trust and the sense of support and collaboration and partnership to do an investment club. But you might have friends that will. You don't have to limit the opportunity. If we're smart, we will create a whole new movement of Black investment clubs. This is a great way for us as a community to attack the historic wealth gap.

Overcome Lack of Trust and Risk Aversion

It is possible that our mentality has become subconsciously entrenched in the Black psyche due to the large-scale betrayals and setbacks Blacks have historically suffered whenever they attempted to invest or save. The Freedman's Bank was an enterprise chartered by the federal government to train and encourage former slaves to save and invest their money. At its peak, it had 29 branches from Pennsylvania to the Deep South. However, it failed in 1874, leaving thousands penniless.[18] W.E.B. Du Bois believed the loss of the Freedman's Bank resulted in the Black community's thoroughly ingrained skepticism and mistrust in banks and the importance of savings as a concept, one that perhaps has been passed through generations.[19]

While my hope is to get as many Black people as I can to embrace *the culture of money* ideology, I fear when it comes to ownership and investing, the elephants in the room are the lack of trust and risk aversion. I'd like to discuss one at a time.

To model the Chisolm family, you need a circle of trust. If you really want to get to the root of it, we don't put our money together and invest with each other because we don't trust each other.

I have heard so many negative comments about Black people *from* Black people. Success has allowed me to walk in many circles, from the sanctified to the secular, with all kinds of people. And having come from the 'hood, I've been able to integrate and communicate with 99% of the Black community, including the "Black elite."

I've disassociated myself with some uppity Black people whose attitudes towards the Black poor seem increasingly conservative and negative. I'm sure you've heard others make remarks like, "Oh, I don't deal with Black contractors, doctors, bankers…" about their own people in a way that they almost sound like racist White people! But it's not just the well-off folks, I've also heard Black people in poverty talk about each other that way, even when it comes down to dealing with Black businesses; hinting at their lack of professionalism and timeliness. And while some of our brothers and sisters struggle to adopt Black excellence, it seems like far too many of us are willing to give in to issues of distrust versus working as a community to move us ahead together. This is another result of internalized racism and exactly what white supremacy wants.

Lack of trust destroys most families. How is it that the other ethnic groups can work together to invest and own? They have trust. Are they born with it? No! They have grown up with it as part of their culture. Likewise, we need to make trust part of our culture. "I am my brother's keeper" needs to be more than a line Wesley Snipes says in the movie *New Jack City*, but something that is at the core of the Black family.

You would think it would be more intuitive to trust each other and work together to get ahead, especially since most of us live in the lower strata of the 99%. Yet, survival mentality breeds selfishness and mistrust so each individual goes down his own path, making the struggle harder.

The same thing happens with many couples' finances. When there are two people on different pages, oftentimes they don't even trust each other to have joint accounts anymore. If you can't trust each other enough to open a bank account together, it will be much harder to build wealth. Even strangers form businesses and create bank accounts with all the owners' names on them. They don't even live together but understand as a principle that money works better together than apart—the more the merrier!

The other issue that often arises is risk aversion. This means we need to take more risks in life. I think our struggle has caused many of us to play it safe, which will not get us very far. To make money moves we will need to take risks. To build circles for pooling money, we will need to take risks. Risk is emotional. Risk is financial. Risk is not reckless if its calculated. The risk I'm talking about has nothing to do with jumping off a cliff to prove to yourself that you are not afraid of heights. I'm talking about taking a risk to succeed.

There is no success without risk. All risk brings reward. The higher the risk, the higher the reward. The lower the risk, the lower the reward. You will never be able to buy property, own stock or open a business if you are risk averse. Listen, we don't all have the same risk appetite and that's okay. The minimum risk we need to take is in building vast networks of relationships in the Black diaspora. By pooling our resources and intellect, we will be better able to take risks and invest in property, stocks and businesses.

It's reasonable that fear settles in if life has been hard. But the only way to have an easier life is to begin to take more risks. One of the reasons I love the Old Testament Bible stories is because there are so many stories about people who took risks to believe God for more. It's just that simple. The Lord's plans for us are good, not without struggle or suffering, yet good. God takes a risk every time He associates his good name with our questionable behaviors. Yet, he has permanently associated Himself with the Church. So, we need to walk in that image and likeness and be risk takers, faith walkers and big believers. I'm not encouraging you to be silly but mature. No risk, no reward. No reward, fewer dreams come true.

Owning more is committing to a strategy of asset appreciation. To value owning property, stocks and businesses that have the greatest potential to appreciate more than we value "status." You cannot leave a good financial legacy if you have no assets to pass down. I hope you will join the community in the goal to *own more* so that we have the ability to *pass down more* to the next generation.

SEVEN

Don't Pass on Passing More Down

F amily, this is the right time for us to have a very important conversation. If generational wealth transfer was a race...we would lose. Trump's rhetoric and behavior have made it clear – rich lives matter most to him, especially White lives. I'll repeat this message until it overtakes your spirit – an economic tsunami is heading our way! The most significant wealth transfer in history is lining up. With the transmission of that money comes power and privilege. Are we really going to trust that the next generation of rich White people are going to do right by Black people?

Sure, there have been models and examples of the rich White people who have considered our plight, such as the White Americans who helped found some of the best HBCUs. Howard University was named after Oliver O. Howard, a White Union officer who led the federal Freedmen's Bureau after the Civil War. Spelman College was founded by two White teachers from Massachusetts, Sophia B. Packard and Harriet E. Giles. And some of its early benefactors were John D. Rockefeller and the family of his wife, Laura Spelman Rockefeller. But historically, as a group, White, wealthy Americans have not used their wealth to uplift Black people. Nor have they used their power and privilege to advance Black people. It's only recently that a discussion of White privilege was brought to the forefront. As of today, if wealth transfer were a race, we'd lose terribly. We must become part of the excellent wealth transfer.

American doctrine claims that we are all treated equally and that we just have to keep working a little harder; put in a few extra hours on a job working for the man and you will get ahead. However, although that appears to be an easy solution, it is not solely where our issues lie.

I can't say it any plainer than this: Asians and Whites have assigned assets and planned ahead to provide a legacy for their children with money, businesses, homes and then some. Meanwhile, Blacks and Hispanics are not planning for legacies or leaving their money or assets for our own children. This is the wealth gap in its purest form. The gap will only increase if this no-legacy-planning trend continues. We can argue all the factors and public policies and make all the prayers we want, but nothing will change until we change. The struggle is real for every Black family.

> Your money culture must maximize the opportunities and resources you have in this life so that you can leave the earth with a richer legacy.

First of all, I tip my hat to you. Look what you have been able to do in your life despite all the obstacles. Imagine what you could have done if you had a head start or a better head start provided by an inheritance. Imagine how well you could be doing if you were taught financial education in and outside the home. It doesn't matter whether you are single with no children or married with five children; the principle is the same.

What can you do to be more intentional about how you will better the lives and integrity of your family and community that come after you? Some say it takes intergenerational communication and valuing the wisdom of elders. According to Renee McCoy, Ph.D., a lecturer at the University of Washington, Seattle, "Family integrity refers to processes through which men and women receive a sense of positive self-worth and value as they become elders. It develops through meaningful intergenerational communication in which the knowledge and wisdom of elders are welcomed and heeded."

Even if you have not been given the best opportunities, what is your reality?

- Are you making the necessary decisions, sacrifices and choices to provide better opportunities for the next generation?

- Have you been working to save money for your family?

- If you are single, have you been making plans to have a family? If you are in your 20s, have you made plans for your 40s?

- Have you been ensuring that, even if you cannot afford to give your current or future child access to higher education, you are giving them the skills and training necessary for scholarships?

You have to live with intent or else no matter what you do, there will always be too much room for error.

The enemies of this movement are short-sightedness, immaturity, selfishness and the laws of survival. It is in our nature as humans to seek for ourselves and our desires of the heart before attempting to uplift, please and encourage others. The simplicity that selfishness gives to us as individuals makes behaving selfishly one of ease and comfort.

Survival works in much the same way. Our nature calls for "survival of the fittest" and "may the best man win (implied by his own effort)." These callings can harm Black people more than others, especially since we are starting from a deficient position.

It is selfish to live in the most prominent house and not be able to provide the next generation with college savings funds because you lived in too much house. It is short-sighted to wear the most beautiful clothing brands when you are young and then miss out on gains in the stock market because you have no money left over to invest.

Your financial immaturity may come back to haunt you when you reach your 70s and still need to work because you won't have enough money to survive on your fixed income.

It is selfish to live your whole life without a care about money only to die broke and leave your closest relative with a big funeral bill that is not his responsibility to pay.

Of course, you may not be this kind of person, but many short-sighted, well-intended Black folks are missing the big point: the small number of wealthy legacies left among us don't lie. We are way behind!

Following the research behind a recent report by Inequality.org, Blacks are held to an income standard of 30% less than that of their White and/or Asian counterparts. This has come about through years of other ethnic groups turning a blind eye to the inconsistent and unequal treatment of men and women of color. With that being said and with all the supporting evidence that they will not change for us, it becomes imperative that we implement the changes ourselves.

The change cannot just happen within your family, but within your church, community and beyond. This problem is not one of singularity: it is one that controls the dynamics of us all and must be treated as such. You know the old adage, we are our brothers'/sisters' keepers, and we must all look to pass along a better life for those like us instead of waiting on someone else to do it for us.

When I was a kid in church, I always heard that "prayer changes things." Can I get an Amen, church? You could also argue seeing Black people being *the culture of money* is an answer to prayers of our forefathers. It will change a lot of things. It will please God.

As I previously stated, the U.S. is on the brink of a $68

trillion wealth transfer. Most of this money will be inherited by individuals, but not much will be disbursed among the Black diaspora. It's time for us to get in this race, overcome like we always do and win as the underdog. We've done it before, and we will do it again!

Turn Your Heart Toward Legacy

I bet you think the one thing you need to do to leave a legacy is start saving money or perhaps, begin investing to grow rich. Maybe you think it's to buy a life insurance policy or start living with margin so there's something left over at the end of each month. What if I told you that the first step to leave a legacy has nothing to do with any external actions? There is only one thing you need to do to start building a legacy.

When I ask this question in my workshops, people start blurting out external actions they believe are needed to *pass down more* while skipping over the elephant in the room. What they all miss is the internal shift that needs to take place in their hearts. The issue is not how much money you have to leave a legacy; it's how much heart you have to do it. Yes, you. What is in your heart for *passing down more?*

A primary heart-felt driver for accumulating wealth sounds something like, "I want to be able to bless my loved ones..." or "I want my kids to be able to..." or "I want to change the world with..."

Leaving a legacy is less about money moves and more about heart moves. If you do not have the heart to leave a legacy, you won't. Sadly, not enough Black people have the heart to make the necessary lifestyle adjustments and resulting choices to make legacy a reality.

I get it. For years, I felt that building and leaving a legacy was solely about money. Most of what I read and heard when I was in my 20s implied that you needed to get rich to leave a legacy. Therefore, throughout most of my young life, I wasted time and money because I assumed someone from my background couldn't and shouldn't be worried about the business of prosperous folks.

I was a pawn of my own making. Perhaps you are too. If you think legacy talk is only for the top 1%, you are falling into the same trap I did. Moreover, the next generation of your family will be further behind their peers.

The wealthy pass down money mainly because they want to ensure a legacy. In America, we have a lot of new money – wealth created over the past 20 years. Most of these new-money folks establish estate plans, make investment moves and purchase life insurance products to make sure wealth transfer happens. They have a heart and won't allow poverty to be associated with their family.

Internal motivators are linked to what's in your heart; that you have the heart to do something for someone else beyond yourself.

My momma, Emma Salter, is the #1 reason I am a success today. I wanted to be able to bless her. I wanted to buy her houses and cars and give her as much money as she would need whenever she needed it. Praise God, my sisters and I have been able to do just that. But while Emma was my #1 success driver, she was not my #1 legacy driver. A legacy driver is the internal motivating force that moves you to *pass down more*. It's the "what's in your heart" thing and the "why" behind the reason you are legacy building in the first place.

Even after achieving some success – which for many Black people is being the first generation to graduate college and get a well-paying corporate job – I was not thinking about legacy. I was blessing momma but not making money moves for the future. At 21, I was young and dumb, all flash and no substance. I was making more money after a few years in Corporate America than both my parents were clearing together. That's how I ended up bankrupt by age 21! If I had discovered a legacy driver before I turned 21, I would probably have done better with my paycheck from day one!

Where There's a Heart, There's a Legacy Driver

Without a legacy driver, you think about today but very little about tomorrow. Your behaviors are not tethered to any great cause, so you take actions that hurt your ability to *pass down more*. So many people live life without a legacy driver. By the time they discover it, it's too late to do anything about it. Without a legacy driver, you will spend, spend, spend and live paycheck to paycheck. The brands we favor will gain all of your investment dollars. They get to survive, thrive and live to see another day while your family will most likely pass down nothing but poverty and pain. You need to identify your legacy driver, otherwise you will be driving some corporation's legacy.

If I had *the culture of money* at age 21, I would have discovered my legacy driver sooner. The good news is my bankruptcy helped me see beyond myself. It forced me to deal with the fact that I was literally worth less than zero. It is complicated and emotionally disrupting to be told in a public space by a judge that you have failed at life. At least, that's how I felt. Despite my college degree and corporate job, I was worth nothing.

Sometimes, we don't change until we've been forced by circumstances that are usually preventable. We are often the ones most responsible for our own failures.

- I pray you don't have to become bankrupt in any area of your life for you to change your behaviors.
- I pray you won't have to experience losing a loving spouse to divorce before you improve.
- I pray you don't have to be fired perpetually before you start to realize it's you and not "the man."
- I pray you will not have to experience the fatal setbacks of making wrong decision after wrong decision before you start praying regularly for guidance.
- I pray you don't experience bankruptcy in any area of your life. Trust me, it's not the right place to be— psychologically, spiritually or experientially.

It was during this period of my life that I married Terri. We were and remain wildly in love. Yep, wildly. I love this Black woman like air. That's for another book – but I must let you know how I feel about her because finding your legacy driver is about tapping into and taking advantage of a "feeling."

Terri and I started making babies literally from day one. We were married in 1995 and my oldest son Dejahn was born in 1997. We had children so soon into the marriage that we didn't even know what it was like to be a young, untethered couple. We didn't live together before marriage, so we had very little in the way of a "getting to know each other" period as spouses. Looking back, we wish we did. We don't regret having children, but we do acknowledge the value of uninterrupted romance. My kids were busting in on our activities during our 20s, which is prime time for lovers! But I digress.

Dejahn was, and remains, an incredibly handsome guy. He was a beautiful baby, and that's not just my opinion. Everywhere we went, people gawked and said he was a looker. The truth is, Dejahn's arrival forced me to deal with something that I had hidden deep inside. From the time we found out we were going to have a boy first, I panicked. I couldn't sleep. Anxiety, which I suffer from time to time, almost killed me.

When the doctor looked at the ultrasound and said you will be having a boy, Terri was excited, I was stunned. Why? I had to deal with the fact that I had no clue and was not well-prepared to take care of anyone.

The idea of Dejahn forced me to deal with the fact that it was only a couple of years before that I was bankrupt: I could barely take care of myself as an adult, forget about taking care of this baby boy. His appearance in the womb forced me to deal with the fact that I might break him. Yes, Black men break things (and sometimes, the people they love) mostly because we were not nurtured by other men to care for others. At best, we get lucky and do it right, but often, we are clumsy with people or downright destructive. Broken people break people. In so many ways, I was broken, and I was afraid of breaking Terri, Dejahn and soon thereafter my other children, Destiny, Dorian and Davin.

I was nervous about raising a son and providing for him. Yet I was excited by the prospect of doing something extraordinary for him and my family. So, while Emma was my #1 success driver, Dejahn was my #1 legacy driver. Looking into his eyes, I knew I'd have to do better in every area of my life; become a better version of myself. I'd have to work harder, save more, invest wisely and become financially educated. Otherwise, I would be instrumental in setting up this kid to fail.

Of course, finding your legacy driver doesn't guarantee you will leave one – you still have to make certain moves – but it does give you the heart to change your behaviors and attitudes about money and life.

I hope Dejahn doesn't read this book because he is the family troll and will make sure he assumes all the credit for everything good that has happened with our family finances. I can hear him saying, "If it wasn't for me, you'd be broke" or "If it wasn't for me, you wouldn't even be an entrepreneur," and so on. The funny thing is, he would be kind of right. Having my first child awakened in me a new level of Black consciousness. With his first breath, he became part of our family's narrative in America because this is what I knew:

- I knew this country would not be fair to him
- I knew his Black skin would threaten white people
- I knew his name, "Dejahn," was far too Black for White people; they would know he was Black when reading his name on a job application
- I knew he might be discriminated against and not even get the interview because his name sounds Black, just as a recent Harvard study proved this bias
- I knew no matter how hard he worked, as a Black man, he would probably receive less than equal pay compared to his White peers. He would earn approximately 87 cents to every dollar his White peers receive, even if he worked twice as hard and was better educated[1]
- I knew that even with his hands up, he could be killed just because he was Black

All of this knowledge came crashing down on me when I heard Terri and I were having a boy. I had to navigate the implications of his Black future when I was just 25. He wasn't going to make it unless I changed. Likewise, there is no future for your Blackness unless you change.

My first son forced me to think about the long-term and less about today. I had to make sure I helped him reach adulthood with a sense of Black privilege by providing him help to offset the disparate impact of his Blackness in America. It didn't stop there. Shortly after Dejahn, Destiny was born in 1998...yes, just one year later. I told you we were wildly in love. Plus, there was too much good music. Then Dorian and Davin were born. While they weren't my #1 legacy drivers, my additional three children were undoubtedly numbers two through four!

Turn Your Heart to the Future

There is a beautiful verse in the Old Testament that speaks to the thoughts I've shared with you. It is prophetic. It is a word for our day and about family. It has implications for legacy. Malachi is a book that acts as a bridge between old and new. The prophet Malachi records the following promise of God: *"And He will turn the hearts of the fathers to the children and the hearts of the children to their fathers..."* (*Malachi 4:6*).

This verse speaks to the healing of a generational disconnect. It speaks to what we need. What God needs. What our legacy needs. For there to be a prophetic call to turn parents' hearts to their children, something must be wrong with the parents' hearts. The verse assumes that the parent and child are not face-to-face but back-to-back. In other words, their hearts are a distance away from each other. I envision hearts turned away from each other as a picture of division, disconnect and coldness. Your heart turned away from your children is a cold position to hold. Back-to-back means you can't see each other and if you can't see them, you can't care.

It's hard to care deeply about things when you don't see them. Every day we throw away more food than some countries need to survive. Yet, because we can't see the starving, we are not moved. It's only when the commercial airs or you take that mission trip to a third-world country that you can see your brother in hunger. That's when you desire to embrace his plight. It's only when we are turned toward each other that we can see each other. It's only face-to-face that you can then allow your heart to meet your brother in a warm embrace.

As a parent, God turned my heart to see my beautiful Black children. I had to turn away from myself, my self-indulgence and self-gratification to see what they needed. They needed my sacrifice. I had to turn my heart to see their education needs, practical needs and social capital needs. Something has to happen on the inside before you can reap the benefits of your behavioral changes on the outside. What do you perceive when you look at your children? Don't have any? Then what do you see when you look at your future? Turn your heart!

Make the First Turn!

Please reread the Malachi verse over and over again. It's rich in revelation. Note the order of the turns – who turns first and then second. The verse indicates that the first turn is not the children's responsibility; it's the responsibility of the parents. I believe the order is intentional. This is not just legacy revelation; it's a family revelation.

There are grown men and women who are emotionally wounded simply because their parents refuse to turn. Because of the hardness of their hearts, the parents will never own up to what they did. They won't own it, apologize or reconcile. Because they don't turn, they leave behind the wrong kind of legacy—brokenness. They don't turn financially either, so the result is generational broke-ness. I'm tired of seeing Black folks in brokenness and "broke-ness." There is a difference between being broken and being broke, though they are related. A broken person does not have to be broke, per se, but usually a broke person is broken.

Families are being ruined because of the hardness of hearts. They don't discuss important things. They keep pressing forward in dysfunction rather than turning financially or otherwise. They can't see each other's plight and refuse to acknowledge each other's story.

If you are a parent, it's divine law that you are to turn first in every area. Your future is your child. Unless you set your heart towards the future, there will be nothing for your prospect to prosper from. That just makes sense, doesn't it? Children don't ask to be here, so you must do what needs to be done for them. Yet, it's not that simple. The Almighty calls parents to turn first, so this text is a window into how He feels about the first generation. By demanding parents turn first, He's making it clear whom He trusts with the responsibility.

You will not *pass down more* if you refuse to turn your heart toward your children. They are your future and will help you see further down the road. As I said, my kids were my #1 legacy driver, but having children isn't the only driver. Some people are driven by leaving an imprint on the world, their community or the businesses they build. I know many entrepreneurs who are young and don't have children, and don't ever plan on having children, yet they have discovered legacy drivers.

I know one young tech leader who is married to her venture. She's secure in the fact that right now, her company is her marriage and her children. As a Black woman in tech, she is driven to survive, to do the extraordinary and, most importantly, to build a business that survives. She has made moves – not to sell, but to scale. Her long-term plan? Be too big to fail. I hope she makes it. She has a good chance because her heart is turned toward something positive.

You will have the passion, endurance and faith to do whatever your heart is turned toward. If your heart is set toward self-indulgence, then there is no legacy in your future. If your heart is turned toward legacy drivers, then you will have something to pass down.

I see businesses, ministries and families fail, not because of the resources they've had, but the focus they did not have.

They made financial moves for what was happening today and missed tomorrow. Malachi is for people with sight who can tap into the next step.

Become a Forecaster So You Don't Need GoFundMe

The culture of money is about having proper financial sight. I'm speaking to you about what God wants to do in your life, but your heart must receive it. To *pass down more*, your heart needs to turn toward something other than yourself. If you do, then one of the blessings you will receive is that people will start to turn towards you. Turn one is the heart of today's generation moving toward tomorrow's generation. Turn two is the heart of tomorrow's generation turning toward them.

I like to think that my children are going to take great care of Terri and I when we are old. We believe in the promise of Malachi 4:6: that by considering our children, God will cause them to feel us. No matter how much we disagree or disappoint each other along the journey, as long as our hearts are turned toward our children, God promises to keep us in their hearts.

Isn't this really what we all want? When we get in the public Black pride space and shout about the restoration of the Black family, it's a slow movement because the first turn still needs to happen. God is waiting for us to turn.

This Black wealth gap is serious. It's an economic tsunami that will sweep through tomorrow's Black generation. If this generation doesn't turn, God help them! If you think Black people are struggling now, wait until you see tomorrow. It's time to turn! Then, and only then, will you see something you need to see. Then and only then will you discover your legacy driver.

The turning of your heart has nothing to do with how wealthy or poor you are. The verse does not indicate that only people with money can and should turn their hearts—it applies to all people. Leaving a legacy is not about how much money you have but how much heart. Big-hearted people leave a rich heritage and not necessarily monetarily. Small or cold-hearted people leave behind a GoFundMe page.

There is no sadder moment being a Black pastor in a Black church than dealing with a family after their loved one has died, and they have no money to bury him. The loss of a loved one often takes a back seat to who will pay for the funeral. Neither the people above nor below the ground had the foresight to make a plan for that day. So, like many who have come beforehand, the family has to "raise money" to give their loved one a proper homegoing. Members of the community try to rally together by giving what they can, even if only support and a meal, while others throw cookouts intending to bring in donations. Family members contact their friends, and of course, the church comes together with calls of assistance during services so that the saints can bring in funds as well. It becomes a time of togetherness, sure. But the unsureness of how the family will pull things off is an additional stressor that they don't need, especially at that time. It is the result of living with no plan. It never fails that there is no shortage of people who are dressed exquisitely at the funeral, but very few of them are considering their own future financial matters.

And don't get me started on those families who want to throw an extravagant send-off. They'll go out and spend massive amounts of money on a new outfit and some jewelry for the deceased, on top of the fact that they choose to finance expensive caskets, posters, flyers, the fanciest of obituary service booklets and more. Imagine that you have made the decision to plan ahead for your passing and choose to do it as large as humanly possible. So, with your nest egg, you and your loved ones prepare catered menus, gold caskets and frivolous additives. The late Bernie Mac said it best: "Why I wanna keep you around for, you're dead and you cost me money. We gotta have four days for this, we gotta have the visitation, the wake, the funeral and the burial. Black folks, we something else. That wake messes me up the most. Where you gotta go in there, sit in front of a coffin and just look at it."

Death is a difficult thing for the family and friends of the one who has passed, but it also reveals the truth about who was living for legacy and wasn't. How you die says a lot about how you lived. Die broke, lived broke. Die well, lived well.

If you don't buy into these culture-saving moves, you will not pass down anything except debt and dysfunction. You will have another one of the GoFundMe funerals. People seem to think that once they have passed away, all their debt is forgiven. Not so! But this idea has been so frequently misconstrued that creating a GoFundMe page for a deceased loved one has become the norm. A GoFundMe funeral is the most significant evidence that the deceased didn't think about the people who would have to bury him. It doesn't take a lot of money to plan for your funeral, just the financial savvy to get a small burial policy to cover your expenses and the discipline to pay it every month.

What makes it worse is those GoFundMe pages do not always get the amount of funds necessary for the whole payment of funeral costs, casket or even a headstone. Why would you dare to leave behind a mental health crisis for your loved ones? The burden of raising money for your funeral will cause an emotional turmoil among them because your final matters will not be in order. If you do this, it means you are too selfish or ignorant to realize what they might experience after your passing. Doing this proves your heart is turned away from them and not toward them.

An associate had a sudden death in her family. Her mother died. However, this acquaintance was only 16 at the time and had just bore a daughter. Not only was she stressed because she didn't know why her mother left her, but this young woman also couldn't figure out how she would pay for a funeral, or even where to start. For the first two days, she called around trying to find estranged aunts, uncles and grandparents to help. Nobody stepped up.

Finally, she received a piece of mail addressed to her. Her mom had actually planned ahead. She had taken out an insurance policy for over $10,000. This young lady was able to hold the funeral and still pay rent on the apartment for the next three months. Her mother had made plans even though they were painful to realize. At the funeral, the 16-year-old stood up and after praising her mother's life, let everyone know just how thoughtful her mother had been by leaving that insurance behind.

I submit this question to you once more – what will people be saying about you and what you left behind during your send-off? Will they testify of your self-sacrificing actions? Will they state how well you set up the family? The truth is, some of our funerals are not just sad because we lost a loved one, but because of the fights and begging that cause more trauma. Let's all move away from the trend of GoFundMe to leaving behind the necessary funds and a plan.

Legacy Requires a Spoken and Written Vision

Once you've identified your legacy driver, then you need to focus on a plan. Dream it. Say it. Let everyone in your house, business and church know that you are leaving a legacy. Then write it. Some people do this in the form of vision boarding. Some just commit behavior change in their hearts. This book's earlier chapters gave you the keys to what to do after you turn. Since we are talking about *passing down more*, you need to start with financial education. That's why we adopt *know more* as our first cultural value. Then of course you can't pass down what you don't own. So, the second value is *own more*. Those are your big to-do buckets.

Now that you are ready to turn your heart and discover your legacy driver, focus on what you should be passing down, so your vision is clear and intentional. It's not enough to *pass down more* money. You must pass down vision and values. *The culture of money* must become multigenerational. The way to pass down vision is to communicate and document it. My theory is that until it's written, it can't happen.

There used to be a time when it seemed every Black person had an oversized King James Bible sitting in the middle of the living room coffee table. It was placed where everyone could see it. If you remember like me, it was probably burgundy with gold-etched pages. It was a cultural statement of our faith to overcome the struggle. It did not matter whether you were a sinner or a saint, if you were Black and not Muslim, you probably had this Bible.

It was something you wanted to pass down. Likewise, you must do something with the values in this book. They should be passed down from generation to generation – *know more, own more and pass down more.* The message is simple, clear, culturally significant and easy to communicate to the next generation.

The idea of being intentional and having a plan is of utmost importance. Three things must be passed down – vision, values and money. It is essential to understand their overall connection.

Vision is what you see and wish for the next generation to do with the resources you leave them. The idea sounds like, "I'd like you to make sure you invest in real estate with the money I leave you," or "Wisely invest the money I leave you so you can *pass down more* wealth to your children."

Values are the set of beliefs that establish the culture of your family. They can be as simple as, "We always help out each other when money is tight," or "Never loan money that you can give."

It is essential to leave vision and values with any money you pass down. Leaving money to a person with no value system is not a great idea. Likewise, leaving money to a person with no vision provides little opportunity for a successful wealth transfer.

I am challenging you to commit to adapting *the culture of money* into your family dynamic. Adapt its values, share them and hold everyone accountable to them. Then articulate your vision clearly, so that your legacy is secure.

Throughout the history of America, the wealthiest families have attempted to do this exact thing. The families that still survive are those that have successfully transferred vision and values to the next generation, besides loads of money. Remember that wealth transfer is more than money transfer. Along with transferring wealth comes the transfer of power and privilege. The next generation needs to understand that they are receiving power and privilege, no matter how large or small and what to do with it.

I'm tired of talking about White privilege. We need to start working on Black privilege. We need to develop our culture for the long game, starting with our generation. We need to pass down a vision for the future and cultural values that will ensure we always have a seat at the spiritual, political, cultural and economic tables of America. Black privilege begins with passing down *more* – including vision, values and money; not just one, but all three.

No Matter What, You *Will* Leave a Legacy

No matter what, you will leave a legacy. The question is whether it will be a good one or a bad one. You only get to choose the result while you are living. If you do nothing about leaving a legacy, then by default you might leave a bad one. While we can't control some things that we pass down to our loved ones, we can be more intentional about the process.

Any reasonable person should understand that leaving a legacy is not optional. We will all leave one whether or not we want to. The chances of you leaving a good legacy by accident are slim to none. Life just doesn't work that way. If you don't plan to leave a legacy, you won't leave a good one.

The problem is that most people die with regrets about what they could have done better, and many times it comes down to money talk. When

> If you don't intentionally set your heart toward leaving abundance, you will leave behind poverty.

most people are near death, their two biggest regrets are the relationships they damaged and the money they wasted. On one end of the spectrum are those who leave behind poverty with broken relationships. On the other end are those who leave behind abundance and reconciliation.

I believe poverty passes down through the heart and through culture. We have been prophetically called to change. I am not saying that external forces don't contribute to poverty; it's just that many of us are modeling behaviors that are harmful and fiscally foolish. We are living life with no plan for the future so, culturally, we may pass down poverty without even trying.

What we are seeking to do in this movement is the opposite. We want our positive financial behaviors to be as culturally influential as our hair, design, dress, language, music and everything else. Black people *are* the culture. And now we must also become a culture of money. Forget *passing down more* of the poverty mindset, even if it is by accident. We need to embrace the mindset of abundance and legacy.

Eighty-year-old Ms. Ethel is on a fixed income. She hasn't worked full time for years, but still maintains a part-time role as a crossing guard. I can hear her saying, "I don't want to sit around the house." She has two simple goals in life: finish paying off her house and leave it to her grandchildren. She is, and has always been, intentional with her plan. She's communicated it and documented it.

Ms. Ethel once told her firstborn, "Son, I know you went through some ups and downs, and I know you went through some challenges. One thing I'm proud about is that you went out there and faced it. You went out there and rode some of those waves son, and I'm proud of you. And I know there are more waves you're going to ride, but I want your children to see that you came through. I am paying off this house for them, so they know that even in your struggles there is the glory."

This is how you spread a money culture by design. You intentionally communicate your plans and wishes. You also model the behavior that shows you are serious about what you are talking about.

Let's get this right. Ms. Ethel's goal in death – even if she does nothing else – is to pay off her house and leave it to her grandkids. And do you know what? Her house is already paid off! Her actions rejected any mentality that said live for now and don't worry about tomorrow. You, too, need to reject any hint of avoiding the struggle.

If you have only received one message from this book, it should be that you know the code to financial healing: start to *know more* (become a money master), so you can *own more* (real estate, businesses and equities), so you can then *pass down more.*

Think about this, Ms. Ethel paid off her house. This presumably took 30 years and according to her son, she may have been late on her payments here and there, but she never lost her home. There have been a few recessions over the past 30 years, but she never lost her house. Why? She had a vision, she communicated it, and more.

A great number of Black Americans' homes were foreclosed during the Great Recession, but Ms. Ethel never lost her house. She never had a professional white-collar job nor made anywhere near a six-figure salary, but her priority was simple. She had discovered an internal motivation. She knew her legacy drivers. So many people have made good money but blow it. Our generation is sick. In many cases, when you get cash in your hands, it disappears—fast!

At one time, Ms. Ethel's son started building an addition to his house after getting a nice salary bump. She asked him, "What are you doing this for? You don't need more room, do you?" He came up with reasons that made sense to him. He later admitted that he expanded the home because it was a statement that he had "arrived." But Ms. Ethel stuck to her culture of money and asked him, "Why are you doing this? Don't make much sense to me. Seems like you have all the room you need!" This was her way of communicating to him that he was not walking on the path of cultural values she had established for the family. She feared her legacy was in jeopardy.

Pass something down. That's what Ms. Ethel is doing to challenge the wealth gap in her family. If we can make this action universal, we will win. My prophetic mission is to secure a sound financial legacy for Black people; to make good money habits part of our culture. In Ms. Ethel's eyes, this was simple. Ms. Ethel lived as a simple, good steward and role model for the generations that will follow her. Live *your* life to pass something down to your children and grandchildren (generational wealth). Live within your means, so that this is possible. Be intentional.

Young Adults – Own Your Legacy, Too

This legacy conversation is not just for old Black people; it's for people of all ages. The sooner you begin to work on your legacy, the better. If you are in your 20s or 30s, you are in the best position to start thinking about your legacy. Your youth is an advantage. It means you have more time than people my age to make big things happen in your life. Like the kid who dreams of the NFL at eight years old, start putting in the work so the vision comes to pass. You must begin to eat, drink and sleep with the idea that will become your legacy.

Please don't think I'm writing you off if you are in your 40s or older, like me. There is still time to shift your life from just living in the present moment; pivot toward living for a possible moment in your future! That's what legacy living is all about; living for a future moment and all of its potential made possible by your sacrifices today.

My goal is not to make you feel bad if you can't pass down anything but to challenge you to engage a desire, regardless of your age. Commit to passing down more wealth to the Black children of the future.

Black people love eating their Thanksgiving meal, but who doesn't really love eating those delicious leftovers, right? When you have a taste and expectation for snacking on your favorite leftovers, what's the worst feeling in the world? Finding out – after you search high and low in the fridge – that some other sneaky family member got to it first and ate the last morsel (And worse, he was probably the one who ate the most substantial portions all through the day!). Of course,

I used to do it all the time to my sisters.

I am a candied yam fiend. Nothing could alter my behavior more than anticipating feasting from a pan of my Mom's incredible yams! There was one Thanksgiving where I almost got sick from eating her yams. There was half a pan of leftovers in the fridge, so I woke up early the next day thinking, "Yum, yams for breakfast." Everyone else was sleeping late because soul food leaves you comatose. So, I had time for another healthy helping of yams for breakfast and even a snack before everyone was awake.

One of my sisters, who also loved yams, finally awoke, and was witness to my selfish actions. She opened the fridge screaming at the same pitch you've probably heard in your house as a kid, "Who ate all the leftovers?" She was noticeably upset and rightfully so. She knew it was me, and immediately began to charge me with being greedy and selfish. Of course, I had to sit through her description of how she was dreaming about eating a plate that morning and woke up with a strong taste for yams. She even acted out the taste-in-your-mouth sound we all know and love.

At that time in my life, I had a blatant disregard for anyone else's happiness. I lacked the common decency to simply poll the family and ask, "Does anyone else want leftover yams?" That simple, forward-thinking act would have made me a hero instead of the Thanksgiving villain. Even then, my heart was turned away from my family and toward myself, which is why I ate all the yams.

If Black people, young and old, don't get serious about

leaving leftovers for someone else, we are going to cause more pain and anger in the future. People will look at us and curse us for consuming everything. They will think of us as unthoughtful, selfish, greedy and ungrateful. It's infuriating to be connected with the actions of selfish and inconsiderate people. I know it's tight, but it's right. If you are committed to selfish acts, no personal growth and can't change your behavior, you can't be *the culture of money*. If you don't turn in the right direction, there will be no leftovers.

Legacy living is living life in a way that creates a margin, using that margin to create wealth, then using that wealth to create a legacy. It's about paying it forward for our own children and our people. Our forefathers did it, so can we. Every adult, young and old, must *pass down more*.

Make A Plan To Retire

Guess what? If you can't afford to retire, then you probably can't afford to leave anything behind. Keep it simple. Your first legacy goal should be to enjoy a proper retirement. Your second goal should be to plan your retirement in a way that you leave some assets to your children. To do this, you will need to work with a financial planner to forecast your retirement income and expenses.

The age-old axiom is true, *"He who fails to plan, plans to fail."* It is also true that God created you with a plan to live your best life. To live by a financial plan and believe you will be wealthy is faith without works. Many well-meaning people worship on Sundays but violate scripture on Mondays. Anyone who fails to plan is being disobedient to their divine design.

The first objection I often hear from many people is that financial planning is "stressful," so they don't do it at all or do it poorly. Others think planning is an inaccurate science or that it takes too much time.

People are conditioned to move away from pain to pleasure, so short- term pleasure is the first choice of many. Thus, buying is easier than planning to buy since it feeds our short-term pleasure need.

Every hard-working person should dream about retiring and reaping the benefits of a life before death without stress. Even the priests in the Old Testament were required to retire at a young age and live well for their service to the Lord's people. Is there anyone in America who deserves a great retirement more than you? Most of us will never live this dream unless we create and execute a financial plan to get us there.

When we were 23 years old, Terri and I went on our first vacation to Orlando, Florida. We couldn't afford a real one, so we did the time-share hustle vacation. Timeshare companies still send mailers or robocall to offer three to four days in sunny Florida if you attend a sales pitch. The one we received was $399 for four days, including coach airfare if we just committed to a one-hour presentation. We spent our early years in marriage traveling on what I call timeshare coupons. We knew how to say "no" after the presentation was up, so it was easy. Besides, we were just coming up from being broke!

On this first vacation, we noticed that most of the people who owned homes and were of retirement age were older White people. We drove through one community dreaming about one day owning a vacation home and we saw old White people golfing, old White people cycling, old White people fishing, old White people power walking, old White people dining...I think you get the picture. These old White people we saw everywhere were smiling and living the life.

I turned to Terri and asked, "Do Black people get to retire and live the good life?" It was a serious question that tormented me because most of the images that we can conjure up of old Black people are not the same. Even after so many years have passed, I still see only a few of us living the retirement lifestyle compared to our potential to reach this goal.

Our grandmommas still help take care of our kids. Many of our granddads are still working, trying to survive on a fixed income that has not kept up with inflation. Even the ones who are blessed to come from the generation of workers who receive a pension or who own a home can barely maintain paying the taxes. And even if they get a vacation, it's usually to visit family or take the occasional cruise if they are able to save enough.

I determined the day we saw all the old White people enjoying retirement that I would be the happiest old Black man on the golf course, cycling, power walking or dining out daily with Terri. We agreed that we wanted to retire young and live a good life until our last days. The issue is, we don't want to be the only Blacks living the dream. I want to see us all prosper! We still have time to make the shift, dream, plan, execute and repeat.

To retire well, you must start dreaming about it, planning and executing. Without a dream and a plan, you are prone to the downfall of shortsightedness and wastefulness. The best way to curb spending splurges is to get a dream that satisfies them more than the dopamine released by a shopping spree. A dream with a plan forces you to consider the cost of future happiness for present satisfaction. This is called opportunity cost; the hidden cost of the financial decision you make today in respect to how it will play out tomorrow.

Retirement Planning Is Paramount

Every financial decision you make either takes you closer to your long-term dream or pushes it further from reality. "Not thinking about it" may put you in an early financial grave. Living life without a financial plan is a mentality I know all too well. Yes, there was a time in my life when I was the least qualified person to write about *the culture of money*. It was my "live for today, take-home pay" mentality that caused me to delay investing my money. Rather than make a decision that was based in logic for my long-term benefit, I made an emotional, short-term decision based upon how much money I had in my pocket from every paycheck. I had no plan yet. I filed bankruptcy. I failed to plan and planned to fail.

Chubb offered employees free financial planning, which I never took advantage of because I was ignorant. Chubb offered Q&A sessions and like the sister I mentioned earlier who wasn't comfortable speaking up, I didn't ask questions because I was too embarrassed. I did what many of us do, smile and wave just like the silent penguins in the movie *Madagascar*. Even though the Lord delivered me from bankruptcy, my lack of planning set me behind many of my White peers who had a plan from day one to retire well.

I remember overhearing a few of them laughing about how they were killing it in the market and how much money they had invested. Some said they had saved nearly six figures. In my early 20s, I filed for personal bankruptcy while many of my Chubb colleagues had widened the wealth gap by investing.

My sin was the lies I had embraced: *"I'll get to that later"* and *"I have time."* Sure, through lots of prayer, revelation, breakthroughs, increased financial knowledge and hard work, I've been blessed to overcome my error. I do not want you to suffer the penalties of financial sin. Do not become financially destroyed because of your lack of financial knowledge.

Having financial knowledge will lead you to living under a financial plan that may definitely get you to retirement.

Moreover, your heritage demands that you become one of the best financial planners.[2] If you want to build a more blessed life, you need to start with dreaming, planning, executing and repeating.

A Financial Plan Gets Your From Retirement Dream To Reality

How much will you need to retire and live well? The answer depends on a few factors, but mainly, the lifestyle you desire to live in retirement. The general rule-of-thumb today is that you can live off 4% of your investments for X amount of years. The first step in financial planning is for you to assign an age for your dream.

At what age do you want to retire? How long do you expect to live after retirement? What lifestyle do you dream of living? These are the most important questions to ask yourself since they will allow you to back into how much you will need to execute your plan. For example, a 30-year-old making $75,000 a year who wants to retire at 50 (many millennials want to retire at 35!) has 20 years to work and save money for retirement at 50. If he expects to live to 90 (which is not out of reach with the advances in healthcare), then he needs 40 years' worth of money to live a certain lifestyle.

Depending on how lavish or reasonable his lifestyle dream, he will need more or less money. Let's keep it simple: retirement is a fancy way of saying, how much can you afford to pay yourself so you can live a certain lifestyle when you decide to stop working.

Let's say the 30-year-old decides that he can only afford to live off $50,000 a year in retirement. Perhaps his plan includes having his mortgage paid off. Since he has no kids to bail out in the future. At $50,000 a year, he expects to be able to travel well and enjoy life with few bills beyond medical costs.

The math is easy: 40 years of life expectancy after retirement multiplied by a $50,000-a-year lifestyle equals $2 million. There are many tools out there to help you calculate these figures, so you don't have to be a math genius to start dreaming and planning. Almost every financial website offers retirement planning and investment returns tools. Some of the best websites I would recommend are Fidelity Investments (fidelity.com), PersonalCapital.com and Bankrate.com. Using these tools, the 30-year-old would need to begin saving 70% of his current salary today. Of course, this seems impossible unless he plans to live at home with his parents until retirement!

As you can see, each individual's financial plan must be adjusted to live the dream. His options include:

- Creating a side hustle and banking 100% of the money he earns for retirement.

- Planning to work longer and not retire young at 50. He will then have fewer years to pay himself in retirement.

- Plan to live fewer years by eating heavily fried, processed foods, salt and sugar. He may not make it to 50, anyway.

As it stands, his plan is probably unrealistic. Notice, I did not mention anything about counting on payments from

Social Security. While these funds are part of a retirement income strategy, relying on it may have you living beneath the poverty level in the future, especially if it's your only plan. The calculations above assume a 7% return on the money you invest during your working years and a 4% return in retirement. You can adjust the numbers using online tools until the calculations work for you.[3]

Let's assume the 30-year-old gets the revelation and decides to work until he is 65 with the same 90-year life expectancy. Using an online calculator with his $75,000 annual salary, he would need to only invest 17% toward retirement each year to live to 90 years old with a $50,000-a-year lifestyle. Don't get lost in the numbers: challenge yourself to get the revelation. By working longer, the 30-year-old would achieve the same retirement lifestyle. Of course, if he gets more than a 2% annual pay raise, earns bonuses, inherits money or creates a lucrative business, he could save even more.

A good steward makes a plan. Gaining knowledge leads to revelation, which leads to breakthrough actions. After reading all this, have you written your long-term financial plan focused on your dream lifestyle in retirement? Or are you planning on dying broke and living your last days regretting your wasted youth?

Create a plan now. Stop reading. Do it now! It's critical that you do. Setting a long-term dream for your life will allow you to effectively communicate and set up the next generation for their future. If you are in a comfortable financial position, that's great! If you are repairing your money situation, share that with your children. Your plan will help you stay focused.

Get started on dreaming, planning, executing and repeating. Sit down with a certified financial planner, not some random dude wearing a shiny suit. Find a qualified financial professional from a reputable firm to help you build a more detailed plan after you dream up the basics. He or she won't judge your financial situation, and some don't charge for a consultation.

Remember these keys for retirement:

- **Invest a portion of your income** during your working years for the purpose of adding to your retirement funds, or put a portion of your hustle money into an account for this purpose
- **Plan to get rid of debt** – including your mortgage – as quickly as possible, preferably before you retire
- **Invest early and wisely.** Consult with a financial adviser who can help you plan for your future

The power of *knowing more* is that it will drive you to plan. Then you can start to live a financially healed life where you *own more and pass down more.*

We've got an unequally yoked society where the income gap keeps growing. Age and race discrimination on job sites often goes unnoticed. And unfortunately, we continue to see people of color working past retirement age rather than enjoying their later years on the green lawns of their local country club.

There is possibly a disconnect in how we see ourselves versus the way that God sees us. Are we meant to not have access to the finer things because, "That's just the way it is"? Or have our selfish lifestyles caused us to be unable to attain these things, let alone pass that attainment down to our children? Does this current state of reality suggest that we are living to bless others?

When looking at this scenario, where do you think that you fit into the problem and what are you doing to become part of the solution? Do you have the full grasp of what the problem is and how you can change in order to circumvent continued inequalities in your own family?

Make Sure Your Papers Are Right

Almost everything in life happens by a plan. Our creation was designed, not random, accidental nor chaotic. Likewise, in you lies the ability to plan and be intentional. Without intentionality, there will be nothing passed down. Which leads me to a simple action for you to take as soon as possible. Get your legacy papers straight! Nothing in your heart or head will happen unless you make sure these documents are filled out and put away for safekeeping. Just in case you forgot, let me refresh your memory – your papers are the legal documents you need to execute your legacy plan. My goal is to get you to take the final action steps and get your papers right. No matter what the amount you intend to leave behind, you will need a will, a medical directive and perhaps a trust.

Everyone should get their important papers in order and in a place your loved ones can find them before you pass because without them, anything you leave behind without instruction will be a mess. The people you don't intend as beneficiaries will fight the hardest to get your money and worldly goods. Yes, the fool at the funeral who will fall all over the casket (and is probably the reason you are in the coffin) will be the first in line to play "snatchies!" Without your papers in order, there *will* be a fight. Just look at what happened surrounding the deaths of Prince and Aretha who left no instructions behind. No papers equal lots of arguments.

I am not a lawyer nor is this book intended to give legal advice. But if you are planning to leave a significant amount of money, you need to consult with an estate attorney to determine the appropriate trust documents that will ensure your vision will happen.

Any credible estate attorney should offer you a free consultation (so don't fear to schedule an appointment). He should also provide a flat rate instead of charging by billable hours for this type of work. Some offer a sliding scale. That is great as long as the top end of the scale doesn't start too high. If you require something extremely sophisticated, it could cost more. Still, most of us aren't leaving behind billions, so a basic plan might just do for you.

There are nonprofit organizations that offer free estate planning, so you have no excuse not to move forward. I have one of the best estate attorneys in the country and she only charges $1,500 for a complete estate plan. It doesn't matter to her how much or how little you have in assets. I only share this number with you as a barometer, so you don't get taken advantage of in the marketplace.

There's another important point that I need to highlight. Remember when I challenged you to find your public voice? Don't be ashamed about what you don't know. The first time Terri and I met with an estate attorney, I felt embarrassed by the questions she asked us. Internally, I felt like her questions exposed my lack of foresight or lack of success. But it wasn't about her questions; it was about our pride.

We stumbled through the same insecurities that many of you may be struggling with now. After about five minutes of us either being coy or positioning our answers to make our situation sound better than it actually was, Lisa, our attorney called us on it. I'm glad she did. We needed to kill the idea of being fake. We needed to stop lying and talking like we had it like that when most of us don't. We need to stop acting like we are right when we aren't. Be real or be undone.

Lisa frustratingly said to Terri and I, "Guys, I'm here to help you create a legacy. If you don't keep it real with me, I can't help you. There is no shame in my office. I have created estate plans for some of the wealthiest people in the Northeast and believe me, they have problems too. Stop comparing yourself in your own heads to what you have or haven't done so we can focus on what you are trying to do."

Wow! She called us out and it was just what we needed to open up and be real. There were people we wanted to leave our money to (and those we didn't) and she wanted us to stop beating around the bush. We had to trust her. There are more millionaires in my home state of New Jersey than many other places in the country and they, too, had to deal with the drama that impacted their estate wishes. So will you.

The key to meeting with an estate attorney is to be transparent and to know what you are trying to accomplish. Don't be fake. Don't lie. Don't save face. Do you want to ensure the next generation is college educated and you can afford to make that happen? Do you want a family business to perpetuate? Do you want to be generous to a church or a cause? Whatever you discover as your legacy drivers can be translated into actions upon your death (or before), but only if they are in writing.

The reason many of us don't talk about legacy is that most people don't like to think about death. But legacy is more significant than death. If you are intentional and start early enough in life, you will live out some of your heritage. Legacy is about the impact and imprint you make on others.

The NBA has something called Living Legends, which highlights former professional basketball players who are celebrated as living legendary performers. They are observed because they are alive and the NBA wants them to know that it appreciates the impact they've made on the game. Discard the idea of legacy being "death talk" and embrace it as "life talk." We should aim to get recognition and acknowledgment while we are living. You don't have to wait until you die. Whether you start working on your legacy at 21, 41 or 61, your efforts will not go unnoticed. Someone will bless God for you because you blazed a trail for them to have a better future.

There is no excuse for anyone to die without properly executed papers. It's just lazy. It is also inconsiderate and cold. The turning of your heart will drive you to accumulate not only wealth, but to protect your wealth with paperwork. I'm just priming your pump to do the right thing. You will need to dig deeper into this topic to figure out the right moves for your family.

Commit to turning your heart to something or someone other than yourself; discover your legacy drivers; and get your papers straight. If you die with your papers right (e.g. established will, trust, medical directive), it means you not only lived well; you made sure your final wishes were known in writing. Then you will be well on your way to *pass down more.*

Life Insurance: The Legacy Hack More Black People Need

Often at workshops, it's the elders in the room who have the most magnificent hearts and want to leave something behind. They are also usually the ones with less education and more meager means. Yet, they have the biggest heart for legacy. God bless our Black elders. I love them.

Many older people are on fixed incomes. Oftentimes, I must encourage our elders that it's not too late for the over 60-year-old individuals to get their estate papers straight, so that they too can leave a legacy. Our elders are often surprised to hear me say that meager means are not an impediment to what is in their hearts.

Once a lady, whom I will call Mother Johnson (we all know someone like her), asked, "I don't have much, but I want to leave my grandkids something (her legacy driver), so what can I do on a fixed income at 70 years old? I feel like it's too late for me." I could see the pain, shame and embarrassment in her eyes. She looked as if she was questioning her whole life and contemplating whether she had failed. Talking about money is hard because money is very much connected to our emotional well-being, so it's really hard talking to Black people about money, because we are so often emotionally drained and challenged.

I was so proud of Mother Johnson for asking that question, especially in a room full of 30- to 40-year-old attendees making way more money than she ever could (yet many of them were basically broke). Meanwhile, she owned her home, which she had paid off 10 years prior. She had lived paycheck to paycheck with no assets to show but an overused bag. God bless Mother Johnson and her heart. I affirmed her courage and reassured her that her heart was in the right place and that if she had only 24 hours of life left, that's all the time she needed to leave something to her grandchildren. Her face went from sour to all smiles. I shared with her the cheat code for *passing down more*. It encouraged her faith and I hope it does the same for you.

The cheat code I shared with Mother Johnson was life insurance. This is not a sales pitch and I'm not trying to throw my weight, even though I have one of the most highly recognized African American success stories in the commercial insurance game. Okay, so I am throwing my weight, but only to help you feel comfortable with my credibility. I know what I'm talking about. I would not be a multimillionaire without being a success as an insurance broker. So, let me pull back the veil and help you prosper.

Life insurance is not a waste of money. It is a hack for legacy money. So many people are under-insured or not insured at all. They are missing out on the easiest no-frills way to *pass down more* wealth. Many reports coming out of the life insurance industry acknowledge that Black people are severely under-insured compared to other ethnic groups. It's like the rest of America has figured out something we haven't.

The reason most of us don't buy insurance is that we don't understand how the coverage works. Insurance is merely the trading of risk. That's it. Whether you cover your life, property, car or business, you can pay an insurance company a premium to take over that risk of loss. This means that buying insurance will always be cheaper in the long run than bearing 100% of the damage yourself. It's cheaper to buy car insurance than it is to pay for a total loss on your car after an accident. Likewise, it's cheaper to pay an insurance company a small premium in exchange for protecting your family from the loss of income and potential assets if something terrible happens to you. And there are definitely ways that you can hack the legacy game and buy yourself a legacy.

I have to be real here. I fear some people might take advantage of this hack, and use the funds set up for legacy to bail themselves out. I hope that your heart really turns and you decide to live like you want to leave a legacy. I hope you live life with margin and invest that margin into appreciable assets (as we discussed in the last chapter). Yet, I can't deny that insurance is such a no-brainer that even if you spend everything you earned in your lifetime on yourself but paid your insurance premiums on time, you would still be able to leave a financial legacy. Selfish living might damage some of your relationships and tarnish that legacy, but your loved ones would not be able to deny that you left them something in the end!

So, I told Mother Johnson that there were products with smaller death benefits designed for elders in her situation. Although it wouldn't be millions, if she could afford a low monthly payment, she could get an insurance policy to leave something behind and rest her heart. I even shared with her that these types of policies rarely require going through a medical exam. She was excited to speak with a life insurance agent. But she was still not sure how she would pass down her property. Her plan was just to die and let her kids decide what to do with it. I cautioned her to consider meeting with a nonprofit organization that could help her set up a will to keep the house out of probate and put down her vision on paper.

Let me share just a few more ideas concerning life insurance. Whole life, variable life and annuity products are very sophisticated and expensive tools that most people should not partake. They have specific-use cases but are not well-suited for the masses. For example, I bought a whole life policy when I was younger, but my market investment account has outperformed my whole life variable product by leaps and bounds.

There is a reason why super wealthy people put more money in the stock market than into whole and variable life products. They know that those types of products are more like investments than insurance. Remember that. Historically, insurance investment products underperform the market drastically and have higher fees associated with them that can eat into returns.

The reality is most of us can afford a pure insurance product, term insurance, with a little tightening of the belt and some foresight. This is the type of insurance I believe 100% of Black families need. It might be the best hack for us to cut into the wealth gap. Term life insurance is significantly cheaper than whole life. Cha-Ching!

Terri and I have used a "staggering strategy" in purchasing our term life products. We buy the same amount of term every 10 years as our incomes and savings increase. This means we are basically turning our term insurance into whole life insurance, but at a much lower cost. This approach frees up our capital to be invested in the market for higher returns.

Using the staggering strategy, there will never be a point in our lives where we will die without life insurance coverage. We could own policies that overlap for ten years, which means that while our health is at its best, we keep pushing out the term. Term simply means the policy's expiration date, which is set in the future. If you die *before* it expires, your beneficiaries get the proceeds (death benefit). If you die *after* it expires, the insurance company keeps all the premiums and beneficiaries get nothing. To offset this risk, Terri and I stagger our insurance purchases.

Here's how it works. Let's say at age 30 you purchase $1 million in life insurance for a term. So, a 30-year term carries you to the age of 60. Then perhaps you purchase another $1 million in life insurance at age 50 so that new term policy would take you to age 80! If you die before you turn 60, you would leave behind a legacy of $2 million. If you die after age 60, you would leave behind $1 million. The older and unhealthier you become, the higher the cost for any life product. Buying 20 more years of term insurance at age 50 is much less expensive than applying for the same $1 million policy at age 60.

Whatever type of insurance you purchase, be sure to use a broker who can shop for the lowest price at the best return, since companies that only represent their own products are usually less competitive and often have higher hidden costs.

Another word to the wise, make sure you get in shape,

lose weight, stop smoking and live a healthy lifestyle before applying for life insurance. You will most likely need to pass a medical exam and the underwriters will review *every* medical record available, including your primary care doctor's notes on your health. This means the underwriters will see every time your doctor suggested that you stop eating pork or lose 20 pounds. The best rates are given to healthy people. So, I don't care if you eat ribs *after* your approval, please stop eating them for three months before your insurance-ordered medical exam so you can get approved at a lower rate.

This may be one of the sacrifices you need to make to leave a financial legacy. You might be in a situation where life insurance is the only way to *pass down more*. It is the cheapest and most effective hack for Black people to transfer wealth, so get started.

The culture of money vision is to see Black America over-insured rather than under-insured for life insurance. Life insurance can be a bailout, especially for those who could not or would not live life with margin and *own more*. So, take full advantage of this insurance hack opportunity. Remember, I don't sell life insurance, I just buy it, so you can trust this advice as objective.

This Will Really Take a Black Village

While there are continuing conversations about the reasons behind the Black population continuing to hold such an unequaled level of transfer expectations, it all boils down to the same thing—we can, we should, and we will do better. Speculation has continued to point to the poor results of slavery, and the passing down of the income gap held by the folks of that era. However, as we continue to grow and evolve outside of that space, it has now become an inheritance issue as well as a community issue.

Take, for example, the facts behind Anthony Johnson and his passing down of wealth to his family. Anthony was an indentured servant who earned his freedom in the early 17th century. He later became a successful tobacco farmer, and one of the first Negro property owners. Many deemed him the "Black Patriarch." All his wealth was handed down to his descendants.

But progress didn't stop there. In 1906, O.W. Gurley arrived in Tulsa where he purchased 40 acres of land with the direction only to sell it to colored people. This land became what is now known as Black Wall Street and was a thriving Black society with an incredible economy before others came in to decimate it. O.W. Gurley was the embodiment of the *passing down more* notion.

So yes, both the lawless stealing of Black-owned property and the dissolution of Black Wall Street have had a lasting impact on the furtherance of Black society. However, while we now have room to grow, we cannot allow institutional racism to weigh us down any longer. Everyone within our community needs to understand the importance of what we will be leaving behind and the essence of what we can do, where money is involved. I cannot overstate the need for us to rally together in efforts to uplift and bless others through the art of *passing down more.* Some studies project that Black people will, as a group, have zero net worth by 2053.

When we come together to aid those who are in our own communities, it showcases a faith and fortitude in ourselves. It also shows others around us that we can do the same things they have been doing for their families and communities for years (while at the same time, neglecting our communities). It is also vital that we change the cycle of poverty by ensuring that we take the proper steps today to help the youth of tomorrow.

After years of selfishness, all too often, some people decide to try to rectify the legacy they want to leave, and unfortunately, their attempts are a little too late. Remember, you don't know the day you are going to die, but you can understand how it will affect your estate when you do! So, every day, hour or minute that you spend waiting for the right time to start will leave a higher possibility that you will run out of time.

This is seen more often with overdose deaths, terminal illnesses that were discovered during the later stages and even untimely murders. Take, for instance, Jamaican-American rapper Bushwick Bill. He was a well-known performer and spent several years living the life of a rapper. In his later years, he announced he was developing a shoe line with all proceeds to be donated to Black youth. Unfortunately, in May 2019, Bushwick Bill was diagnosed with stage 4 pancreatic cancer. He was never able to fulfill those dreams for himself or his community.

Some people have asked why they have not been blessed with the wealth they desire or feel they need, especially since they attend church, tithe, pray and take part in fellowship. This is tricky to answer because sometimes God is waiting to deliver something better to you. It is also possible that you want things that are not within His will. Perhaps you are seeking your will and not His.

While pondering this question, I thought of an inspirational quote from the late Nipsey Hussle. He was selfless regarding his community, in seeking to aid others and in his quest to bless everyone he touched. He said, "We look at life like it's about what you can get from life. I read something and I was like, that's not what it is, you'll always be unfulfilled if you look at life like that. It's about knowing you're going to leave one day. And, you know when you leave, the only way you're going to be fulfilled is if you know you gave everything you had. You emptied yourself here, you left it all here, because it's temporary and you've got a moment."

Sometimes, it is not about what you can do for yourself. It's not even about doing unto others as they do unto you. It's about the development of the family, community and our society as a whole.

EIGHT

The Culture of Money and Black Churches

"If you want to do anything with the Black people in this country, you still have to go to or go through a Black church," according to Jay-Paul Hinds, PhD, Assistant Professor at Princeton Theological Seminary. Dr. Hinds, who also taught at Howard University, is a subject matter expert on the care of self and care of congregation, a general introduction to pastoral theology.[1]

The Church is a living body. Black people are a historically valuable part of the body of Christ. Black churches are Black culture. Their power is immeasurable. They still hold power despite all the rhetoric heard in the media or through social networks. Black churches birthed our way of dress, music, Sunday dinners, education, entrepreneurship, social activism and anything else you can name. Blackness and church are inseparable. No matter how long absent, in the toughest moments Black people find refuge in church. In most urban centers, Black churches are still feeding, clothing, getting the lights back on and supporting the lives of millions of Black people.

I'm alarmed by the number of Black professionals who have found comfort in the last 20 years by worshipping outside the community. There is nothing wrong with broadening your horizons, but many Black professionals left with sharp criticisms of Black churches. Now, they are in no-man's-land since many of the White churches they flocked to have embraced a false theology that Trump is sent by God to heal the land of lascivious liberals!

If the Black churches die, Black culture is over as we know it. God desires churches in Black communities to survive because God loves Black people and He doesn't want to see us without healthy self-esteem and identity.

This is a book about money – but not really. It is a book about Black culture and making it more excellent. We can't do it without the support of the Black church.

How Covid-19 Changes the Game for Black Churchgoers

After the COVID-19 pandemic, leaders of Black people in churches, cannot return to the old ways of doing things. This is a harsh reality, but churches have to deal with it. Yes, non-Black churches with Black congregants and predominately Black churches have to deal with how COVID-19 disproportionately hurt Black people. As a result of the economic fallout from COVID-19, churches are going to experience enormous new pressure to bring hope to the hopeless...especially financial hope.

It is more important than ever to understand what the Spirit of the Lord is saying to the Church. Some of the stewardship warnings from God that have resulted from the COVID-19 pandemic are:

- The earth was given to humanity
- Corporate responsibility includes operating as social enterprises—not taking advantage of workers and consumers, churchgoers and volunteers
- Take care of our lives, including our health, our families and, of course, our finances

Now that the tide has turned, it's critical that pastors and church leaders start asking, "What does it all mean?" Naturally, it means the way churches have been ministering to people in the past must change: not just in worship or online versus offline, but how they disciple people, and in which areas people must be discipled. In the past 20 years, churches have made a significant, positive shift toward attracting more people. But now, I believe there is a shift toward church dispersed with greater effectiveness and influence in the marketplace.

Now churches are forced to embrace and live out. The Church is a body, not just a building. This body of people must be discipled spiritually, relationally and financially even when they can't come to a building. In fact, I would argue that going to church may not be the most significant worry on people's minds right now. People are thinking about how they're going to get through the COVID-19 recession. How are they going to eat next week? How are they going to deal with the unknowns concerning the prospects for their jobs? Will their small businesses make it through this?

Pastors and leaders must begin to turn their hearts toward what God has in store for His people. People have greater needs today. Greater needs demand a greater response from the Church.

The Call to Build People over Buildings

In the last chapter, I asked people to turn their hearts toward their children. Now, I ask church leaders to turn fully toward the well-being of the children of God. For the most part, we have allowed the wealth gap to go unaddressed and unacknowledged in our circles. This issue is bigger than simply preaching about money. When most church leaders preach about finances, they usually cover generosity, tithing and occasionally, stewardship. Their congregations need inspiration, but they also need leadership, and a delivery system to help bring them out of lack—just "sowing a seed" won't do it. As the justice message is finally taking its rightful place in the pulpit, the people, need the Church to come alongside them for true financial healing.

I defend the Church because literally almost everything Black people have is because of its hard work and prophetic leadership. The baton passed from Charles Allen to Martin Luther King, and now to today's leaders to continue to address economic issues within Black communities. Black pastors and white pastors with black churchgoers, also owe the people prophetic leadership in economics, and should become more consumed with building the financial capabilities of Black people.

While I defend the value of the Church, I am critical of how lately its communities have focused on constructing ever-larger buildings instead of focusing more on building up Black people. We have been consumed with attendance numbers and building sizes. I can't count how many times pastors have challenged me to build a bigger building. I can count very few who urged me to focus on building bigger people. Having beautiful facilities are important but how beautiful are we making the people in the pews? Something is wrong with a theology that does not make room for building up financial resources for the people.

Meanwhile, many of the poorest Americans are abandoning the Black church en masse.[2] Research findings by political scientist Ryan P. Burge, Eastern Illinois University, points to the disparity of wealth as an issue. By stepping away from church communities, the people who are most financially strapped also end up losing out on social networks and social capital—which can make their economic situation and outlook even worse, according to Burge.

The sad truth is some pastors don't desire poor members. Many prefer preaching to the wealthy and influential, therefore, all their ministry and programs aim to support and build the community of influence.

It's only a matter of time before the other members of the congregation feel the burn and leave the church. The dominionistic mandate has made the influential member the most coveted commodity in the Church. If you are reading this as a pastor, don't get offended by truth – own it. Be healed and turn your heart toward the financial future of your people. Otherwise, one day you might find yourself as pastor to a group of people with even fewer resources to support your ministry.

Dr. King Started Something That Covid-19 Demands Churches Finish

I'm a big fan and student of the first century church. These people had endurance. They knew how to survive and thrive in challenging times. They adapted quickly and lived out faith practically. The COVID-19 pandemic has forced churches to re-examine how they "do" church in many ways, especially in light of how the virus has negatively affected the communities they serve. The Church has had to figure out the "new way of doing things," considering how a world in crisis benefits from its value.

At the time of this book's publication, the country was (and still is) experiencing great financial pain, and COVID-19 has intensified this pain for Black people. This disparate economic impact on Black people will continue. The reality is that COVID-19 has marked the dawning of a new age for the Church. It has unraveled things, so churches today must shift, like the Black churches did in the '60s. That's when churches fought hardest for Black inclusion in the economic opportunities of America. Dr. King was laser focused on economic empowerment and opportunity for Black people. He demanded the country to consider a more excellent way. In an article for MSNBC, the journalist Ned Resnikoff listed four ways Dr. King radically pushed an economic agenda:

- In 1968, members of Dr. King's premier civil rights group, the Southern Christian Leadership Council (SCLC), drafted a letter demanding "an economic and social bill of rights" that would promise all citizens the right to a job, the right to an adequate education and the right to a decent house, among others

- Dr. King believed that every person was entitled to a livable income, whether they worked or not. In the 1968 book Where Do We Go from Here: Chaos or Community? he called for unconditional cash transfers to every American citizen. These cash transfers wouldn't just be enough to scrape by on, either. Instead, Dr. King thought that a guaranteed income "must be pegged to the median income of society, not at the lowest levels of income"

- Dr. King spent much of his career working with labor unions, while also working to push them in a more radical direction. At the time of his assassination, he was campaigning in Memphis, Tennessee, on behalf of the city's striking sanitation workers. He delivered his final address, the famous "I've Been to the Mountaintop" speech, to a crowd of predominantly black sanitation workers and supporters of their right to form a union

- The very first right to be enumerated in the SCLC's economic bill of rights was "the right of every employable citizen to a decent job." In addition to a guaranteed income for everyone, those who were willing and able to work would be guaranteed a job[3]

Dr. King showed the world that it needed a better way to allow opportunity to all people, but especially Black people. Let's not forget that many Black church leaders were very critical of Dr. King's methods and messages. Many did not allow him to preach in their churches. The National Baptist Convention kicked him out, arguing he was moving too fast. This is what happens when you see the pain of the day and challenge comfort – sometimes people aren't ready.

Regardless, we can credit Dr. King with challenging churches to invest in the fight for, and construct better vehicles for, Black people to prosper. This is a time for brave ministry to a Black population that is suffering its greatest lack since the Great Depression. It's time for church leaders to embrace the fact that this season offers a huge opportunity to be better stewards of Black people. The harvest is plentiful of people that churches can reach and disciple into financial health. But God is looking for church leaders who are not ashamed of the Gospel's expansive reach, and excited about the possibility of seeing a financially healed people.

The Local Church Should Be the Epicenter for Financial Healing

Black people need a financial exodus out of lack and into abundance. I'm sick and tired of every crisis in America affecting us worse than everyone else! The Old Testament concept of healing in this manner is found in the exodus of the Jews from captivity and oppression under the Egyptians. Exodus means "to come out." God turns Moses' heart toward the people in lack, and then gives him a plan to bring them to freedom. In Exodus 3, God defines this healing or rescue as bringing Israel out of Egypt where Jews were impoverished. In this sense, financial healing looks like addressing the wealth disparity in the Black community. That's what exodus is – to come out or to leave a place.

The Old Testament exodus can be compared to the New Testament's concept of discipleship. True discipleship is a healing ministry. A disciple of Jesus is one who trusts and follows Him and obeys all of His teachings. When Jesus said to "go and make disciples," (Matthew 28:18-20), it was a call to model Jesus' example to operate in the same love, the same community and within the same power. Therefore, the only way a disciple knows they are a disciple, is if they can replicate themselves within others. For that to happen, a spiritual healing must take place in their lives. In this sense, spiritual healing and discipleship are aligned with one to another.

Applying these concepts to different areas of life can bring about healing for family and relationships. There's healing spiritually, which is usually the context we think of in terms of bondage and oppression. Then there is healing for financial illness. If people can be discipled into the maturity of walking after Christ, in terms of Christian conduct, Christian character and Christian service, people can also be discipled and brought into a deliverance in finances.

As I mentioned before, financial healing is akin to leaving Egypt and going into the Promised Land, as the pathway from lack to abundance. But as a component of discipleship, it can move people from worldly concepts of wealth abundance, lack in poverty, to a completely holistic biblical concept.

Widening The Ministry Lens

I understand that talking about financial principles to church leaders, may make some glossy eyed, and start thinking of their many concerns. Some concerns are warranted based upon their past dealings with financial gurus and experts who've run through the church only to fleece the sheep. Others disconnect because they feel strongly that financial instruction is not church business. Yet there are others who certainly desire to preach about finances but feel less than capable with the subject matter. One reason I wrote *The Culture of Money* was to inspire churches with Black congregants to develop a response to the economic plight of Black America. I congratulate those churches who used the pandemic to build better delivery systems to connect with people, and yet maintain church budgets. My concern is that with the high rate of change in the way churches are reaching out, they may lose sight of the greater financial vision needed to thrive post-pandemic.

Vision is everything right now. The most attractive vision includes the well-being of the sheep. Sheep follow shepherds because they need to be fed, and live. They need green pastures, and it is the shepherds' responsibility to get them the grass they need. The coronavirus has rewired my leadership focus. It has made me focus even more on "people first." It has challenged and expanded my heart for people. Churches need more than catchy slogans like "faith over fear," which is cute right now, but what are they going to do in three years when Black and Brown people are in a deeper hole? When the Great Tsunami hits? When any and all prospects that Black people had for succeeding are swiped away in a matter of 90 days by a lethal virus? The church needs to reconsider how Black people are going to live and function financially. Church leaders will be challenged to concern themselves with what it means for congregants to pay their bills versus worrying about paying the mortgage on the church.

I've seen a loss of vision in Black churches when it comes to economic empowerment. Some churches will find themselves scrambling when it's too late versus navigating people to greener pastures. So, the question becomes, "What is the churches leadership role going to be on this issue of creating a money culture in Black America?" This crisis should be causing churches to think about the financial well-being of your sheep more than ever. It's during a crisis that leaders provide clear vision along with strategic, tactical and spiritual plans. It's in a crisis that great leaders gain great insight.

The reality is that many church leaders, including me, often spend a lot of time thinking about how to build a better Sunday experience. Pastors lean toward building better facilities, getting better worship teams, having a better band, shining better lights and all the accoutrements of what will attract people to the service. After Sunday morning vision must now be so much more than that. There are many new pressures, coming from economically challenged people, for churches to do more. Churches need to get ahead of the curve.

Post COVID-19, people are going to be more attracted to a faith that includes God delivering and healing people from financial bondage. They're going to be more attuned to that message than ever before. Churches must be able to facilitate discipleship and consider financial healing as part of spiritual formation.

We see this kind of vision in the early church in the

radical economic wealth redistribution program at the end of Acts, Chapter 4. That is where Peter and the Apostles challenge the people to practice the pooling concept, I discussed earlier to address one of the greatest needs of their church—money.

Whatever the plan is, Black churches, from this point forward, should address financial healing for people who are in financial bondage. So much of the Bible is about financially restoring things that were lost, not just spiritually, but physically. As in Joel 2:25, the Bible declares restoration of what the palmerworm and the cankerworm have eaten. What they ate were crops, and crops sold created income for people. Coronavirus is a worm that has eaten the paltry crops of Black America, but I still believe that God wants to restore. He wants to download to Black church leaders His economic empowerment plans to do it. Effective ministry in the 21st century, will require an even greater emphasis on economic empowerment. This is the response to the pandemic expected from both God and Black people.

Financial Healing as Discipleship

Every age requires our practices and methods to change, not theology. The whole church is built on Jesus Christ, His crucifixion, His salvation by faith alone and His baptism into the body of believers. I'm not suggesting that the Church expand or redefine what we believe. But I do think ministry must change to reach the people that God has called the

Church to reach in this day and time. All of its methods must change to heal the 21st century church, which is why I feel that financial healing is a function of discipleship.

Through discipleship in the New Testament, the Apostle Paul addressed the lack in Thessalonica, a very poor region. The Apostle showed the people of Thessalonica how to use their hands to generate income, how to save their money and how to prosper (2 Thessalonians 3). Paul was bi-vocational while ministering at this poor church. He knew how to earn money making tents, and he showed the people how to do the same. He encouraged that church to model its behavior after his orderliness. While in their midst, Paul didn't rely upon financial support from the poor people in a poor church. He commended the church in Philippi for sending him offerings while he ministered in Thessalonica (Philippians 4:16). Speaking holistically, the Apostle John echoed Paul's ministering with this sentiment about the Church: prosper spiritually and in all things, even health (3 John 1:2). For John, this sentiment included the people's financial health.

So, what am I saying? Governments can't solve the wealth gap for Black people. They've had sporadic success in helping us with many issues. God wants the Church to work on this issue. This is the heart of God and He has sent me as a voice in this season to call out and expose all those things that hold us back, so that we can walk in true deliverance and freedom. The healing aspect of discipleship is when you find yourself in a new place provided by receiving and living out the

Gospel. Local churches can cause true financial healing by systematically addressing the negative financial practices and behaviors that keep Black people in bondage.

My lofty goal for *The Culture of Money* is to move Black America into more resources and better stewardship. The Church has been providing financial advice since its beginning. U.S. churches have been offering more and more financial workshops – a relatively new phenomenon. These biblically based programs offer actual strategies that attendees can apply to improve their budgeting, saving, debt, investing, giving, estate planning and other financial topics. Churches, including mine, promote these programs on our websites, in newsletters and even on internally aired commercials before Sunday morning services. But word-of-mouth from the graduates of the classes are usually the best advertisements. A good number of members of the next class are friends and relatives of previous class members. All congregants can use help in reducing debt, handling taxes and creating a financial game plan.

The point I am trying to make is simple, A consistent, easy-to-understand delivery system is needed to provide financial ministries. More churches can join in this movement and become the epicenter of financial healing in the community. In addition to great hospitality, incredible preaching, dynamic worship and great facilities, it would give people a reason to hope and join churches. That's what discipleship does. It causes the healed to pay it forward and own the responsibility to help the brothers and sisters heal (Luke 22:32).

Teaching about finances is not the only solution available for Black churches, and it is not the point of this chapter. Regardless of what system churches create, they need a way to address the systemic lack in Black communities. The dreadful Covid-19 pandemic (which we are in the midst of at time of publication) requires unprecedented leadership and action to help an already disadvantaged people close the gap. If you are a church leader, stick with the biblical mandate to build up people. Build a system and watch how program after program will help your people and make them whole. God gets the glory, but your church will get the credit for solving a problem that no one else is and achieving what no one else can. And the blessings of the Lord will certainly fall upon you. If you are a member of a church, then push your church leaders to develop a response to your financial need.

Churches can leverage the COVID-19 pandemic as an opportunity to help shape people and shift them toward seeing the love of Christ in a brand-new way. How would you feel if the church solved the biggest issue of our day?

A disciple-making process must be inclusive, not exclusive, of financial healing.

This disciple-making process must be a weekly part of a church's regular DNA. It has to be theologically sound and practically utilitarian. If churches shift towards discipleship and spiritual formation with respect to financial healing, it will see the same results as the churches in the 1st century Rome. When they were faced with persecution, they turned the world upside down and thrived in it.

It's time for church leaders to think about the influence and scale of the body, not about the influence and scale of the ministry. I challenge churches to think progressively. Think about how a church can be a part of *The Culture of Money.* Think about how churches can use these values to drive Black congregants towards economic security. Think about life after the COVID-19 pandemic. Think about how it can move people from feeling like they are living in a place of scarcity to a place of abundance.

Black America needs you—the Church—now, and Christ needs Black America. I'm here to help and support churches any way I can.

Meet People Where They Are and Reap the Benefits

Churches must meet people where they are and help them build up to a place where the people *and* the church they support reap the benefits. There is an untapped economic power in churches. There are many pastors, like Apostle Paul, the tent maker, who are bi-vocational champions. They preach at night and work by day, doing tremendous work in some of our poorest communities. I want to thank them for their service. Let's push for a more systematic commitment for financial healing as part of a church discipleship platform. *The culture of money* is a discipleship program that can provide real deliverance through local ministry.

Black churches are still one of the safest places to be unapologetically Black. They are guardians, cultural purveyors and protectors of Black culture. They are best positioned to positively impact the Black community and eradicate financial illiteracy. What a huge opportunity! Imagine if a trip to the church included a brief lesson on entrepreneurship or generating passive income. Imagine if churches required practical financial classes and offered more educational resources to help congregants aggressively pay off student loans. Imagine a church helping congregants learn everything there is to know about money while building their financial capability and confidence by attending financial education classes.

Churches have a real opportunity to use the culture of cash to change the narrative from, "All the preacher wants is my money," to "I have a lot of money because of my church." A financial education curriculum can break down the walls of distrust between the congregation and church leaders. Practical ministry can heal congregants' lives. There is a need for churches with Black congregates to pull up and come through.

Systematic changes like I have suggested might not happen overnight, but let's continue to push church leaders to create more opportunities for financial education and well-being beyond preaching a good sermon on giving!

NINE

The Culture of Money Pledge

The *Culture of Money* is for Black people. It's written for Black people to help save their lives, now and in the future. I'm concerned that we are not taking what we are about to face seriously. Not everyone believes that the future holds cataclysmic events like massive flooding, super storms and worldwide food shortages from global warming. But then, no one on earth could have imagined the devastation that came about worldwide from the pandemic (though Mr. Trump knew about it months before it ravaged the U.S. and did nothing to prepare us). Please believe me, there is a super storm brewing in the form of a financial pandemic. It is coming, and Black people, we need to be prepared! It will hit like we've never seen before since the days of slavery. If we stand by and do nothing, it will result in one group of people ending up with everything and another group, most likely us, with nothing.

We can prepare for this storm. We can be blessed in this storm. But we need to act now! Black people and the Black church, together, unite in solidarity to heal and face this storm head on. This is an issue for every generation of Black people alive today. We must focus more on monetary behaviors and less on monetary outcomes. We need to do the work on ourselves. The government and politicians will acknowledge the problem, but few are brave enough to do what it takes to right a great historical wrong. So, we must do it for ourselves in the very best way we can. In a way that I hope causes great deliverance and healing, I've poured my heart out trying to expose every possible factor that could hold us back.

Let's be clear about the effort it will take for *the culture of money* to change Black America. This effort needs *all* of Black America—churches, businesses, higher education and most importantly, you! To that end, I have compiled some of the most impactful messages found throughout this book for you to remember while taking your financial journey:

1. Adopt a core value to pursue knowledge in all areas of your life, including financial literacy, which will bless your life's space

2. Understand your money-motions and money script so you can make more logical decisions

3. Be consistent, disciplined and faithful to financial principles, and you *will* be able to build your wealth

4. Shift your money-motions, outlook and thoughts. To get what you've never had you must do what you've

never done

5. Understand the money script that auto plays in your head so that you can manage yourself better in the marketplace

6. Visualize the journey, not just the big picture, or you will struggle to live the dream

7. Raise your expectations. If you expect only a little, you will get only a little out of your life

8. Build your confidence and take authority over your financial future by asking as many money questions as necessary

9. Take financial literacy to the next level by using what you learn, or the effort will be worthless

10. Remember – every financial decision you make either takes you closer to your long-term dream or pushes it further from reality

11. Reward Black business with your dollars, especially those owned by Black women

12. Retirement planning is paramount to establishing a proper money culture you can pass down to your

children, and cut into the widening racial wealth gap

13. Know that there is enough money, assets, property and job growth for all of us, if we just show each other how to attain it

14. Build wealth – like most of America – by owning three things: property, equities and businesses; not cars, jewelry and clothes!

15. Know that ownership is everything. Ownership is freedom. Ownership is American. Ownership must be Black!

16. Recognize that being wealthy is not about how much you earn; it's about how much you're worth

17. Turn your heart toward your future and legacy by discovering your success and legacy drivers

18. Make a plan to leave a legacy or you will leave behind poverty

19. Comprehend how financial knowledge can show you how to use your money and finances the *right* way today. It has the potential to shift Black people into a whole new tomorrow

20. The Black church is in the best position to lead on the wealth gap issue. Financial healing is part of spiritual formation and discipleship

21. The churches that build members over buildings will win in the future

The culture of money is an ideology for creating real, sustainable generational Black wealth and I hope you agree it's needed at a time like this. It is a platform to partner with Black churches for Black wealth creation and legacy.

These values are simple and repeatable – *know more, own more and pass down more*. If we can do those three things within our community today and articulate these values to the next generation, we will increase our individual wealth as a community. We will also create enough wealth to have a seat at the table politically, economically and socially. This is what Black folks really need to secure our future!

Poverty can be generational, and my heart aches to think about the future of poor Black people. It's going to take some extreme behavioral change to make the shift, but that's what *the culture of money* is all about.

Please change. Please be accountable for your financial future. I have laid out all the arguments for change and given you the tools to improve. Now it's up to you, and only you can take the first step to make the change.

This altar call is for financial healing. Think about the future or you will perish in it. The good person you desire to be demands that you build a good life and leave a legacy. Praying like it's all up to God won't do. If a future of Black poverty doesn't scare you enough to work like it's all up to you, then you missed the entire point of this book.

Your personal financial education is everything right now. In fact, I think financial literacy in the Black community may be the civil rights issue of our day. We can't fix what we don't know and what we don't know is ultimately hurting us. Take note and remember the many negative psychological behaviors that can cause us to lose out on great opportunities for wealth creation. Increase your confidence with financial and psychological knowledge so you can know more and move forward.

Have you made the shift to leave behind the unbeneficial live-for-today mentality to start moving toward living more purposefully for tomorrow? Have you decided to take action and educate yourself, think like a boss, own stuff and leave a legacy? If yes, then congrats and welcome to the movement.

This positive financial behavioral change is for all of us to accept. If every Black church, sorority, fraternity, social group and nonprofit would get involved, and jump on *The Culture of Money* bandwagon, here's what will happen:

- We will take financial education seriously.
- We will *know more* and no longer look at ourselves to wonder why we missed out on the last significant market boom. In fact, we will *be* the next market boom.

- The average inheritance of white families will no longer be 10 times that of Black families.
- Systematic oppression will have a harder time existing in a world where Black people have economic and political power.

Thank you for waking up to the truth and living your life more purposefully. This is God's plan for you. He wired and designed us to think about the future. He made us with everything we would need on earth to be successful. As you adopt these new principles, your financial behaviors will cause you to live life with margin. Think about it – you will have less financial worry today and tomorrow, so that there will be something left over for the next generation. You are on your way to becoming a bona fide member of *The Culture of Money*.

I pray you live up to your privilege. Let us walk in Black excellence and redefine Black wealth and legacy. We will *know more, own more and pass down more* – that's living *the culture of money*.

My Last Request: Take the TCOM Pledge

One person living *the culture of money* can bring up a family. One family can bring up a community. One community can bring up a people.

The Culture of Money is calling you to the alter of financial healing. Visit thecultureofmoney.com and take the TCOM

Pledge to follow our three principles:

- *Know More*
- *Own More*
- *Pass Down More*

So that YOU can leave an inheritance!

Let's do this together. I'm praying for your healing.

Special Acknowledgments

First and foremost, without God, nothing in my life would be possible. All praise and thanks to Him who leads me.

Most importantly, he has always connected me to the most beautiful people blessings. *The Culture of Money* is no exception. I'm so grateful for the Black excellence involved in this book. Chief among them is my publicist, strategist, and sister, Cordelia Donovan makes big happen. Her cultural insights were invaluable in helping me fine-tune my writing and connect to the broader movement for Black lives. She is joined by Dedra N. Tate, who manages to perfection, always moving things toward the stated goal and keeping everyone focused on the next steps. The excellence of photographer Keith Major and the SGrayUnlimited team - led by creative director and hairstylist Stacy Gray, with fashion stylist Keely Bembry, make-up artist Lisa Jones and groomer Kareem Grant, made me look and feel like a million dollars. There was also a lot of help from a stable of Black writers, graphic artists, and editors. They also want to see Black people living financially healed lives. Without their professionalism and excellence, these words would not have made it to print.

I also want to give special acknowledgment to my wife, Terri and daughter, Destiny, who read and re-read this book from beginning to end at my request. It was a blessing to have such accomplished and published writers at my disposal. It is also great to have fellowship with the most supportive Spiritual family. The sound theological shaping of my spiritual father and Presiding Bishop, Kenneth Ulmer, has been very instrumental in helping merge marketplace success with my ministry calling. It was also beneficial to bounce ideas and concepts off of my spiritual brothers, Bishop Vanable Moody, Pastor Wayne Chaney, and Pastor Jody Moore. These guys never made me feel like I was intruding on their already over-committed schedules. In one of his busiest seasons, Jody read the manuscript and provided valuable feedback that helps me reach pastors of Black churches more intently.

I wouldn't have the time and freedom to do ministry, seminars, or writing without my two "marketplace spiritual children," Rick Grimes, and Charlene Brewer. The executive leadership and growth of my largest company, Professional Risk Solutions, has freed me up to help improve our world. They are part of my journey to create wealth through ownership, and as a result, are on the pathway to join the Black millionaire club.

Lastly, it has taken me five years to bring this book to market. During that time, I saw people in my local church suffering from repeated financial setbacks. They worked hard, loved God but seemingly could not find the financial freedom they sought. The value of their Black lives drove me to pray, study, research, write, and develop the Wealth Track, a program to disciple people into financial health. The value of their lives is why this is more than just a book for me. Instead, it is my contribution to a broader movement that honors Black people and strives to empower them economically.

ENDNOTES AND FURTHER READING

Introduction

[1] Kumar, Manisha. "Difference Between Philosophy And Ideology." *DifferenceBetween.net*, July 28, 2011, www.differencebetween.net/miscellaneous/difference-between-philosophy-and-ideology/

Chapter 1: We Need The Culture of Money

[1] Guilford, Gwynn. "Black Income Is Half That of White Households in the US – Just like It Was in the 1950s." *Quartz*, September 1, 2018, www.qz.com/1368251/black-income-is-half-that-of-white-households-just-like-it-was-in-the-1950s/

[2] Wilson, Valerie. "Before the State of the Union, a Fact Check on Black Unemployment." *Economic Policy Institute*, February 1, 2019, www.epi.org/blog/before-the-state-of-the-union-a-fact-check-on-Black-unemployment/

[3] Ross, Janell; National Journal. "African-Americans With College Degrees Are Twice As Likely to Be Unemployed as Other Graduates." *The Atlantic*, May 27, 2014, www.theatlantic.com/politics/archive/2014/05/african-americans-with-college-degrees-are-twice-as-likely-to-

be-unemployed-as-other-graduates/430971/

[4] Bessler, Abigail. "A Black College Student Has The Same Chances Of Getting A Job As A White High School Dropout." *ThinkProgress*, June 25, 2014, archive.thinkprogress.org/a-black-college-student-has-the-same-chances-of-getting-a-job-as-a-white-high-school-dropout-b7639607fdf1/

[5] "Comparing the Cost of Living between 1975 and 2015: You Are Being Lied [to] and Fooled When It Comes to Inflation Data and the Cost of Living." *My Budget 360*, www.mybudget360.com/cost-of-living-compare-1975-2015-inflation-price-changes-history/

[6] Masci, David. "5 Facts About the Religious Lives of African Americans." *Pew Research Center*, February 7, 2018, www.pewresearch.org/fact-tank/2018/02/07/5-facts-about-the-religious-lives-of-african-americans/

Chapter 2: You're A Slave to Money and Don't Know It

[1] Kenneth C. Ulmer. *The Power of Money: How to Avoid The Devil's Snare*. March 16, 2010, Destiny Image Publishers, ISBN-10: 0768431999. My spiritual father, Bishop Ulmer, eloquently interprets this verse of Matthew 6:24 by pointing out that mammon is money, and we fall prey to making money our God. In turn, we are controlled by money, and do not use it for its divine redemptive purposes. I argue that we fall prey to this

phenomenon because we remain in an undelivered state. We pray, but fail to properly identify the emotions that drive us to feel the need to serve mammon in the first place. So the pattern repeats itself.

2 God continually asked Israel to "consider" and "remember" his past actions, and the implications for his future if his negative behaviors were repeated. These are terms of reflection and decision. The goal of this activity is informational; it is actionable, with the end result being change. Read Deuteronomy 32:29 where God points out the wisdom of those Israelites who properly considered and understood how past actions contributed to present problems. My hope is that you incorporate this message into your daily financial reflections.

3 Church folk should not place their trust in luck, but in God's faithfulness. People cannot claim to have faith, and depend on luck to get them out of financial troubles.

4 Some people get luck and blessings twisted; they are not the same. Luck is based on human chance and blessings are based on divine release.

5 Proverbs 13:7

Chapter 3: Why $1,000,000 Right Now Will Destroy You
1 John 8:31-32

[2] Weinschenk, Susan. "Shopping, Dopamine and Anticipation." *Psychology Today*, October 22, 2015, www.psychologytoday.com/us/blog/brain-wise/201510/shopping-dopamine-and-anticipation

[3] Stewardship is a fancy way of discussing how you manage resources. A steward, similar to a manager, is responsible for how things run within a home, a business department or a personal budget. To be a steward is to accept 100% responsibility for managing away from lack and towards abundance. God favors good stewards; they are a reflection of His care for His creation. As He has managed well the universe, so must we manage our universe well. Stewardship is the true antidote to the addiction of excessive spending, but there is more work to do.

Chapter 4: Own Your Money Truth

[1] Romans 12:1-2, Philippians 2:5 and 1 Corinthians 2:16.

Chapter 5: What You Don't Know Is Killing You

[1] Kusisto, Laura. "Black Homeownership Drops to All-Time Low." *WSJ.com*, July 15, 2019, www.wsj.com/articles/black-homeownership-drops-to-all-time-low-11563183015

[2] Brockman, Katie. "Americans Think They're Smarter Than They Really Are About Money, Survey Shows." *The Motley Fool*, July 1, 2019,

www.fool.com/retirement/2019/07/01/americans-think-theyre-smarter-than-they-really-ar.aspx

3 Investopedia. "The Lottery: Is It Ever Worth Playing?" *Investopedia*, January 29, 2020, www.investopedia.com/managing-wealth/worth-playing-lottery/

4 Natella, Stefano, Tatjana Meschede and Laura Sullivan. "Wealth Patterns Among The Top 5% Of African-Americans." *Impact Series: Credit Suisse Research*, November 2014, New York, NY, www.brandeis.edu/heller/heller/iasp/pdfs/racial-wealth-equity/racial-wealth-gap/top-5-percent.pdf

5 Elliott, Alan R. "What Investing In Stocks Tells Us About The Racial Wealth Gap, *Investor's Business Daily*, March 9, 2019, www.investors.com/news/investing-in-stocks-racial-wealth-gap-connection/

6 "The Lottery: Is It Ever Worth Playing?" *Investopedia*, January 27, 2020, www.investopedia.com/managing-wealth/worth-playing-lottery/

7 John 14:26

8 Matthew 28:19

Chapter 6: Own Or Be Owned

1 "The Freedman's Savings and Trust Company and African American Genealogical Research." *National*

Archives and Records Administration, Summer 1997, Vol. 29, No. 2, www.archives.gov/publications/prologue/1997/summer/freedmans-savings-and-trust.html

2 Gerena, Charles. "Urban entrepreneurs: the origins of Black business districts in Durham, Richmond, and Washington, D.C." *Econ Focus,* 2004, pp. 36-39. *Federal Reserve Bank of Richmond,* Virginia. https://www.richmondfed.org/-/media/richmondfedorg/publications/research/econ_focus/2004/winter/pdf/economic_history.pdf

3 Messer, Chris M., et al. "The Tulsa Riot of 1921: Collective Violence and Racial Frames." *The Western Journal of Black Studies,* 37, no. 1 (2013): pp. 50–59.

4 White, Walter F and Editors. "*Tulsa, 1921,*" *The Nation,* www.thenation.com/article/archive/tulsa-1921

5 Gerena, Charles. "Urban entrepreneurs: the origins of Black business districts in Durham, Richmond, and Washington, D.C." *Econ Focus,* 2004, pp. 36-39. Federal Reserve Bank of Richmond, Virginia.

6 Lee, Trymaine. "How America's Vast Racial Wealth Gap Grew: By Plunder." *The New York Times,* August 14, 2019, www.nytimes.com/interactive/2019/08/14/magazine/racial-wealth-gap.html

7 Bruenig, Matt. "The Top 10 Percent of White Families Own Almost Everything." *The American Prospect*, September 8, 2014, www.prospect.org/power/top-10-percent-white-families-almost-everything/

8 Deuteronomy 1:8

9 Yates, Jonathan. "90% Of the World's Millionaires Do This to Create Wealth." *The College Investor*, February 11, 2020. www.thecollegeinvestor.com/11300/90-percent-worlds-millionaires-do-this/

10 "African American Land Ownership: Ted Turner Owns Nearly 1/4 of What ALL African Americans Own." *Eurweb.com,* October 25, 2015. www.eurweb.com/2015/10/25/african-american-land-ownership-ted-turner-owns-nearly-14-of-what-all-african-americans-own/

11 Kiersz, Andy. "The 20 Biggest Landowners in America." *Business Insider*, April 16, 2019, www.businessinsider.com/the-20-biggest-landowners-in-america-2019-4

12 Rognlie, Matthew. "Deciphering the Fall and Rise in the Net Capital Share: Accumulation or Scarcity?" *Brookings Papers on Economic Activity*, vol. 2015 no. 1, 2016, pp. 1–69. Project MUSE, https://www.brookings.edu/wp-content/uploads/2016/07/2015a_rognlie.pdf

Ultimately, the study concludes that the rise in both housing wealth and housing inequality stems mainly from the increase in the value of land. Whose land do you think has increased in value most? Who do you think owns most of the land that is increasing in value.

[13] Wake, John. "The Shocking Truth 50 Years After The 1968 Fair Housing Act: The Black Homeownership Paradox," *Forbes*, May 19, 2019, www.forbes.com/sites/johnwake/2019/05/16/the-shocking-truth-about-the-u-s-black-homeownership-rate-50-years-after-the-1968-fair-housing-act/#591bb7d263ba

[14] "Fidelity Survey Finds 86 Percent of Millionaires Are Self-Made, *Business Wire,* July 19, 2012, www.businesswire.com/news/home/20120719005724/en/Fidelity-Survey-Finds-86-Percent-Millionaires-Self-Made. According to this study, of those who are self-made millionaires, their top sources of assets included investments/capital appreciation, compensation and employee stock options/profit-sharing.

[15] The "Golden Rule" of Leviticus 19:18 was quoted by Jesus in Matthew 7:12 and Luke 6:31. He positioned it as the second great commandment. The common English phrasing is, "Do unto others as you would have them do unto you."

[16] "Woman-Owned Businesses Are Growing 2X Faster On

Average Than All Businesses Nationwide." *Business Wire*, Sept. 23, 2019, www.businesswire.com/news/home/20190923005500/en/Woman-Owned-Businesses-Growing-2X-Faster-Average-Businesses

17 Jan, Tracy. "Banking While Black: Minority Business Owners with Better Credit Scores Than White Counterparts Face Worse Treatment and More Scrutiny." *The Washington Post*, September 10, 2019, www.washingtonpost.com/business/2019/09/06/banking-while-black-minority-business-owners-with-better-credit-scores-than-white-counterparts-face-worse-treatment-more-scrutiny/

18 Washington, Reginald. "The Freedman's Savings and Trust Company and African American Genealogical Research." *National Archives and Records Administration*, www.archives.gov/publications/prologue/1997/summer/freedmans-savings-and-trust.html

19 Schweninger, Loren. "Black-Owned Businesses in the South, 1790-1880." *Business History Review*, Vol. 63, No. 1, *Entrepreneurs in Business History* (Spring, 1989), pp. 22-60.

The Souls of Black Folk, pp. 1–2, Penguin, New York: ISBN 978-0140189988.

Black Reconstruction in America (The Oxford W. E. B.

Du Bois) An Essay Toward a History of the Part Which Black Folk Played in the Attempt to Reconstruct Democracy in America 1860-1880: W. E. B. Du Bois, Henry Louis Gates, author; David Levering Lewis, introduction, contributor. 9780199385652

Chapter 7: Don't Pass on Passing More Down

[1] Gruver, Jackson. "Racial Wage Gap for Men - Compensation Research." *PayScale*, May 7, 2019, www.payscale.com/data/racial-wage-gap-for-men

[2] We love God. God is a planner. God made plans for Jeremiah's life (Jeremiah 29:11), gave Moses a plan to build the Tabernacle (Exodus 26:30), revealed to Isaiah a plan for the whole world (Isaiah 14:26) and revealed plans to prophets (Amos 3:7). Jesus taught the disciples that no one should try to build a life without counting the costs, i.e. having a plan (Luke 14:28). When applying this teaching to our money, it becomes clear that money planning is both wise and divine.

[3] Find many useful financial calculators online at www.Bankrate.com.

Chapter 8: The Culture of Money and Black Churches

[1] "Welcoming Jay-Paul Hinds." *Princeton Theological Seminary*, November 19, 2019, www.ptsem.edu/news/welcoming-jay-paul-hinds

[2] "Many of America's Poorest People Are Abandoning The Church In Large Numbers." *BCNN1 Black Christian News Network,* Dec. 18, 2019, www.blackchristiannews.com/2019/12/many-of-americas-poorest-people-are-abandoning-the-church-in-large-numbers/

[3] http://www.msnbc.com/all/mlks-fight-against-economic-inequality#49742

*To learn more and to join The Culture of Money
community, visit the author's website at
<u>www.thecultureofmoney.com</u>.*

CPSIA information can be obtained
at www.ICGtesting.com
Printed in the USA
LVHW110733080121
675995LV00004B/118

9 781953 307125